The Best Homemade
Vegan
Cheese &
Ice Cream
Recipes

Marie Laforêt

Robert
ROSE

For complete cataloguing information, see page 139.

Disclaimer
The recipes in this book have been carefully tested by our kitchen and our tasters.
To the best of our knowledge, they are safe and nutritious for ordinary use and
users. For those people with food or other allergies, or who have special food
requirements or health issues, please read the suggested contents of each recipe
carefully and determine whether or not they may create a problem for you. All
recipes are used at the risk of the consumer.
   We cannot be responsible for any hazards, loss or damage that may occur as
a result of any recipe use.
   For those with special needs, allergies, requirements or health problems, in
the event of any doubt, please contact your medical adviser prior to the use of
any recipe.

Translators: John Lee (cheese text and recipes); Donna Vekteris (ice cream text
   and recipes)
Editors: Sue Sumeraj and Jennifer MacKenzie
Proofreader: Kelly Jones
Indexer: Gillian Watts
Design and production: Kevin Cockburn/PageWave Graphics Inc.
Layout: Alicia McCarthy/PageWave Graphics Inc.
Photography: Marie Laforêt
Yellow texture: © istockphoto.com/duncan1890
Circular pattern: © istockphoto.com/ulimi

The publisher gratefully acknowledges the financial support of our publishing
program by the Government of Canada through the Canada Book Fund.

Published by Robert Rose Inc.
120 Eglinton Avenue East, Suite 800, Toronto, Ontario, Canada M4P 1E2
Tel: (416) 322-6552 Fax: (416) 322-6936
www.robertrose.ca

Printed and bound in Canada

1 2 3 4 5 6 7 8 9 TCP 24 23 22 21 20 19 18 17 16

Contents

PART 1

Vegan Cheese

Discovering Plant-Based Cheeses

Cheese with no milk content — the very idea! Is it really possible? Is it any good? Why even eat cheese when the whole point is eliminating dairy products from your diet?

Dairy-free cheeses are an intriguing option whether you are vegan, have lactose intolerance or a milk allergy, are trying to eat a healthier diet or are simply curious about new culinary horizons. These days, vegan cheeses are becoming ever more popular, and in the chapters that follow, you'll discover 25 absolutely stunning vegan cheeses, including recipes to replace the most common conventional cheeses (such as Cheddar, mozzarella, Parmesan, ricotta and feta) as well as some more creative, innovative recipes to inspire you.

About the Word "Cheese"

The Latin term for cheese was *caseus formaticus*, meaning "a molded piece of pressed curd." This gradually developed into the Italian word *formaggio* and the French word *fromage*, both derived from *formaticus* — "shaped into a form."

Is it a misnomer to call a food containing no dairy products "cheese"? In my opinion, "vegan cheese" and "plant-based cheese" are perfectly apt descriptions of this novel formed food, especially as they also involve draining, fermenting and maturing techniques that are similar to those used in traditional cheese-making.

Another term for vegan cheese that often crops up these days is "fauxmage," a pun on *fromage* meaning "fake cheese." I dislike this neologism because it suggests fakery — that vegan cheese is not real food. Vegan cheese is *not* fake cheese, a poor imitation, borderline inedible. On the contrary, plant-based cheeses are real culinary inventions designed to replace animal-derived cheeses in an ethical diet that avoids exploiting animals, or as part of a casein-free diet. In terms of flavor, these are simply different cheeses, with different flavors and textures.

Commercial and Artisanal Plant-Based Cheeses

Vegan cheeses really have the wind in their sails! These last few years, we have seen countless new brands hitting the market. So, are the vegan cheeses in our stores as different from each other as the animal-derived varieties?

The answer is a resounding yes, because, as with dairy produce, you can find both commercial and artisanal cheeses. The ones most readily available in shops (which can also be purchased online) are commercial vacuum-wrapped cheeses. They have the advantage of being easy to ship and relatively inexpensive, and they come in a broad range of flavors and textures, with versions of conventional cheeses as well as some original products that are not trying to copy any known cheese.

What are the drawbacks of commercial vegan cheeses? Many contain palm oil, they are not necessarily organic, and some taste pretty average, lacking both full flavor and the soft freshness of dairy cheese.

However, a mini-revolution in the world of vegan cheese has been afoot for some years now with the emergence of companies offering artisanal products that are fermented and even ripened! In the United States, artisanal brands include Kite Hill and Tree Line Cheese, as well as Dr. Cow, whose cheeses are on sale at a small vegan cheesery in Brooklyn. The writer Miyoko Schinner, who wrote the fabulous book *Artisan Vegan Cheese*, is due to launch a company selling artisanal cheeses in both North America and Europe!

The next big innovation likely to revolutionize the world of vegan cheese, still in its infancy, is the Real Vegan Cheese project, launched by researchers in California with the goal of synthesizing plant-based casein from baker's yeast to create a new type of "real" plant-based milk that will be turned into cheese in the same way traditional cheese is made.

With the growth in expertise and ever-increasing demand, this is by no means the last you are going to hear about vegan cheeses.

A Few Points Regarding Homemade Vegan Cheese

Homemade vegan cheeses are very different from those you will find in stores. While there are techniques for aging them longer at home, you need very special conditions with regards to hygiene, temperature and humidity to ensure food safety and stable results. This is why you will not find recipes in this book for cheeses aged for several weeks in the open air. I have stuck to quick and easy homemade cheese recipes.

Working with plant-derived products, you can manage to create cheeses with interesting textures and flavors that come close to animal-based cheeses. It is best to treat these vegan cheeses as different varieties of cheese rather than as imitations to be compared with the originals. However, in the first chapter, "The Classics, Vegan Style," the goal is to offer handy alternatives to popular cooking cheeses. These are cheeses that are meant to be combined with other ingredients and used for cooking rather than eaten alone — although they are very tasty on their own, too!

The Basic Ingredients

These are the raw materials that form the basis of vegan cheeses, producing a broad range of textures. They are very versatile and have a neutral taste that you can build on with the addition of various flavorings.

Soy Products

Soy milk is the only plant-based milk that can curdle — which is, in fact, how tofu is made, with the addition of vinegar, lemon juice or nigari. So tofu is itself practically a vegan cheese. But this property of soy milk means it can also be used to make soft cheeses, like ricotta.

Regular and silken tofu provide interesting textures, in various degrees of firm and smooth. Soy yogurt and lactofermented tofu add that slightly sour flavor typical of fermented products, while tempeh, a product made from fermented soybeans, has a slightly bitter taste and can be used as a base for stronger cheeses.

Legumes

Rich in protein and with a range of textures, legumes are an excellent base for vegan cheeses. One legume I am especially fond of is the lupini bean, which has a similar flavor to soft cheese, particularly feta. Lupini beans packed in brine are available in jars in the international produce aisle or online.

Nuts and Seeds

Raw cashews (*not* roasted salted cashews!) can be used to make a thick cream after being soaked and puréed with water. Many types of cheese can be created using this basic ingredient, which can also be fermented. Soft cashew purée has a cheesy tang, is handy as a source of fat (very important in cheese-making) and readily blends into a sauce.

Soaked and puréed blanched almonds are used in the same way as cashews. They produce a lumpier, less creamy texture, but are very good for making small, round oven-baked cheeses.

Cheese can also be made from raw macadamia nuts, but given their high price and scarcity, I have not included them in this book.

Finally, tahini, a sesame seed paste with a stronger taste than that of cashew or almond purée, is often used in homemade vegan cheese recipes.

Texturing Ingredients

These ingredients allow you to create various degrees of firmness, with consistencies ranging from very soft and creamy to firm. They each need to be heated to a specific temperature and nearly always need time to set in a cool place.

Agar Agar

Derived from algae with gelling properties, agar agar is used to solidify a preparation. Depending on the amount added, agar agar can help you create chunks of semi-hard cheese or very soft cheeses, like mozzarella. Agar agar must be heated to over 176°F (80°C) so that it can gel as it cools. It will take several hours for the cheese to harden after cooking.

Agar agar powder is available at organic food stores. To use agar agar flakes in place of powder, substitute 1 tbsp (15 mL) flakes for each 1 tsp (5 mL) powder called for in the recipe.

Odorless Coconut Oil

This coconut oil is processed to remove its coconut taste and smell, but it still has the same properties as regular coconut oil and will solidify at temperatures under 77°F (25°C). This means it can be added as fat to a preparation to make a cheese that is both firm and melts in the mouth. Coconut oil must be melted in a bain-marie (a warm water bath) in order to blend in perfectly with the other ingredients, then left in a cool place to set.

Starches

Tapioca starch, cornstarch, potato starch and arrowroot starch all serve the same purposes: binding and, even more importantly, thickening. Each has a different thickening capacity. You will need to heat and stir the preparation for several minutes so that it thickens evenly. (If you cook it too long and it gets a little too thick, you can mix in a bit of liquid, such as water or a plant-based milk, to bring it back to the desired consistency.) When making a runnier cheese, like Cancoillotte or nacho cheese sauce, you may need to blend it briefly if the cheese has become slightly set upon cooling.

Natural Flavor Enhancers

Nutritional Yeast

Stronger than brewer's yeast, nutritional yeast is a choice ingredient if you want a cheesy flavor. It blends in perfectly, even with cold preparations. If you are keen on tang, you can always add a little more than the amount indicated in the recipe. But be careful not to overdo it or you will smell nothing else!

Lemon Juice

Lemon juice adds a sharp and slightly bitter flavor that is lacking in the basic ingredients, while also enhancing the other flavors. Always use freshly squeezed lemon juice, not the bottled variety. But take care not to add more than the recipe specifies; if the consistency of your preparation is too thick, add one or two spoonfuls of water rather than extra lemon juice. Lemon-flavored cheese will not really taste like cheese at all!

Miso

This Japanese condiment, used to make soup and stock, is also commonly used in organic cuisine to flavor sauces and other preparations. The firmness of this soy paste is useful, especially when you're making tofu misozuke. While brown miso is often used to add a meat-like taste to vegan food, white miso, which is the palest and mildest, offers the perfect gentle flavor for cheese.

Spices, Seasonings and Condiments

- **Garlic, onion, shallot:** Use fresh to flavor soft white cheeses and dried powder to create a cheesy flavor. These ingredients should be added before cooking.
- **Mustard:** Sharp and pungent, mustard must be used sparingly. It will spice up and strengthen the taste of the cheese without overly flavoring it.
- **Aromatic herbs:** Use basil, chives, tarragon, thyme, oregano and/or herbes de Provence to flavor soft cheeses or to coat molded or shaped cheeses.
- **Chile peppers and other spices:** To add spiciness or flavor, use according to taste.

Fermentation Agents

Rejuvelac

A fermented drink made by sprouting grains (or quinoa), rejuvelac was invented by Ann Wigmore, a pioneer of the whole-food movement and founder of the famous Hippocrates Health Institute. Rejuvelac is used to ferment oilseed-based vegan cheese substitutes. Here's how to make it:

- **To sprout grains:** Rinse and drain 1/2 cup (125 mL) wheat berries, rye berries, quinoa or other whole grains. Place in a sterilized jar and add enough filtered water to cover by at least 1 inch (2.5 cm). Seal the jar and let the grains soak for at least 8 hours or overnight. Drain off the water and rinse the grains; drain again, leaving the grains moist but not very wet. Cover the jar with a sprouting lid or fine cheesecloth and a metal ring. Lay the jar on its side and let the grains sprout at room temperature (68°F to 75°F/20°C to 24°C), away from direct sunlight, for 2 to 4 days or until the sprouts are about 1/2 inch (1 cm) long. Rinse and drain the sprouts.
- **To ferment:** Add 2 cups (500 mL) filtered water to the sprouted grains. Replace the sprouting lid, or cheesecloth and metal ring, and let ferment in a warm, dark place for 2 to 3 days or until the liquid is a cloudy white and has a tangy flavor. Carefully spoon off the opaque white layer that forms on the surface of the liquid and discard it. Strain the rejuvelac through clean cheesecloth into a clean sterilized jar. Compost or discard the spent grains. Use rejuvelac right away or seal the jar and store in the

refrigerator for up to 1 week. Makes about 2 cups (500 mL).

Sauerkraut Juice

A lactofermented drink used for its detoxifying properties and its probiotic action, sauerkraut juice can also be used to ferment cheese. It is available in bottles at organic grocery stores.

Kombucha

A fermented, slightly tart tea drink obtained through a symbiotic colony called a "mother" or "mushroom" grown with sweetened tea (or a plant infusion). Look for plain kombucha at organic food stores.

Kimchi

This traditional Korean side dish is a mixture of lactofermented vegetables with seasonings and chile peppers. The most popular variety is made with Chinese cabbage. Although kimchi is often made with fish sauce, there are also vegan versions available.

Techniques and Utensils

- **Curdling/draining:** Use a sieve and cheesecloth to drain freshly made cheese. This is done in the same way as for regular dairy cheese.
- **Fermenting:** Fermentation must take place in hygienic surroundings to avoid the growth of dangerous bacteria. So it is essential to use utensils that are spotlessly clean. Sterilized glass jars are preferable to plastic containers.

- **Molding:** Metal rings, small dishes, bowls and a wide variety of containers can be used to mold cheeses, which need to set in a cool place.
- **Drying:** Because aging in the open air is somewhat complicated to arrange at home, the cheeses in these recipes dry in the oven or a food dehydrator. Depending on the recipe, the cheese will tolerate high temperatures to a greater or lesser extent. If in doubt, always keep a close eye on the cheese as it dries.

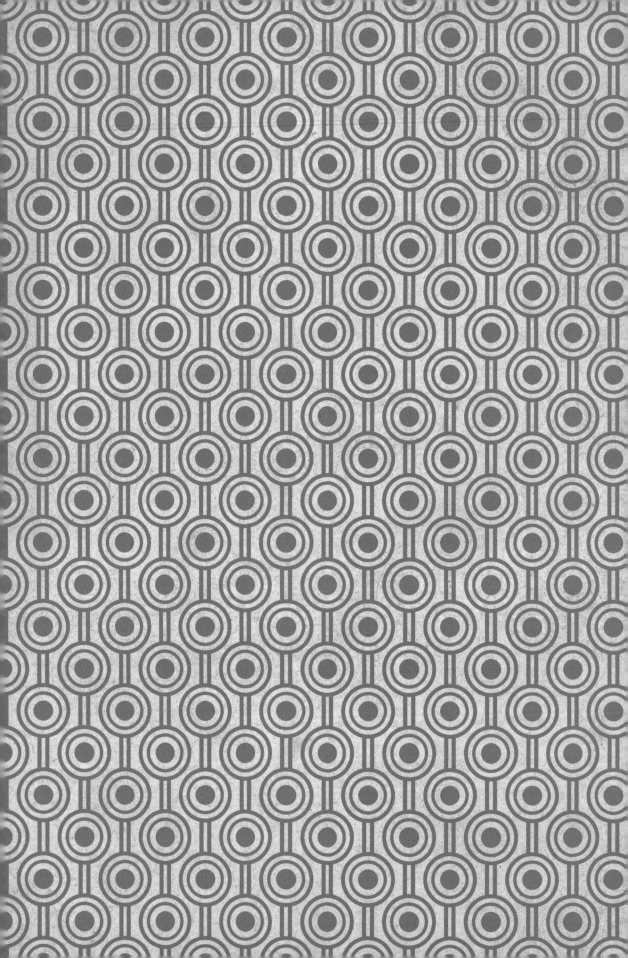

The Classics, Vegan Style

Parmesan

The ideal recipe to get you started, this cheese takes just a few minutes to make, so you can always keep it on hand.

MAKES 1 SMALL JAR

- Food processor

1/2 cup	raw cashews	125 mL
1/2 cup	blanched almonds	125 mL
2 tsp	sesame seeds	10 mL
1 1/2 tbsp	nutritional yeast	22 mL
1 tsp	sea salt	5 mL

Tips

The almonds and sesame seeds make this vegan Parmesan naturally rich in calcium.

For a cheese with an even finer texture, use 1 cup (250 mL) cashews and omit the almonds.

1. In food processor, combine cashews, almonds, sesame seeds, yeast and salt; process to a fine, slightly grainy powder. Use immediately or transfer to a jar or airtight container and refrigerate for up to 1 week.

Recipe Ideas

- Zucchini or eggplant au gratin
- Stuffed pasta shells sprinkled with Parmesan
- *Quick pesto:* Mix a little olive oil and fresh basil with parmesan — perfect with whole wheat pasta and sliced cherry tomatoes.

Cheddar with Roasted Red Pepper

This tasty cheese with excellent color makes an ideal alternative to melted Cheddar in all kinds of recipes.

- Food processor

5 oz	hulled drained brined lupini beans	140 g
3½ oz	peeled roasted red bell peppers	100 g
¼ cup	nutritional yeast	60 mL
3½ tsp	agar agar powder	17 mL
1½ tsp	salt	7 mL
7 tbsp	plain soy milk	100 mL
5 tbsp	melted odorless coconut oil	75 mL
2 tbsp	cashew butter	30 mL
1 tbsp	freshly squeezed lemon juice	15 mL
1 tbsp	water	15 mL
2 tsp	Dijon mustard	10 mL

Tips

Cut this cheese into thin slices or strips before melting.

For burgers, place 1 or 2 thin slices on a cooked vegan patty and broil for a few minutes to melt the cheese.

1. In food processor, combine beans, roasted peppers, yeast, agar agar, salt, soy milk, coconut oil, cashew butter, lemon juice, water and mustard; process for several minutes, until smooth.

2. Transfer to a medium saucepan and bring to a boil over medium heat, stirring. Boil, stirring constantly, for 1 to 2 minutes or until slightly thickened. Pour into dishes or rings and let cool.

3. Cover and refrigerate for 3 to 4 hours, until set, or for up to 1 week.

Recipe Ideas

- Potatoes or cauliflower au gratin
- Broccoli quiche
- Cheddar croquettes
- Quesadillas with avocado, cheddar and cilantro

Mozzarella

A mozzarella that is firm but melts in the mouth, that can be used as is in a salad and yet melts perfectly in the oven? This is the recipe I've been dreaming of for years, and I am delighted to share it with you!

MAKES 2 BALLS, 4 TO 8 SERVINGS

- Blender
- Two 1- to 2-cup (250 to 500 mL) bowls, lined with plastic wrap with 3-inch (7.5 cm) overhang

4½ oz	firm silken tofu	125 g
2 tbsp	cornstarch	30 mL
¾ tsp	agar agar powder	3 mL
¾ tsp	salt	3 mL
⅔ cup	plain soy milk	150 mL
7 tbsp	plain rice milk	100 mL
6 tbsp	plain soy yogurt	90 mL
2 tbsp	freshly squeezed lemon juice	30 mL
⅔ cup	melted odorless coconut oil	150 mL

Tip

This mozzarella melts perfectly and becomes really runny. Hence it is ideal for pizzas, for au gratin dishes and for tasty Welsh rarebit.

1. In blender, combine tofu, cornstarch, agar agar, salt, soy milk, rice milk, yogurt and lemon juice; purée until smooth. Add coconut oil and blend until mixture is thick and emulsified.

2. Transfer to a medium saucepan and cook over medium-high heat, stirring constantly with a wooden spoon, for about 5 minutes or until thickened to the consistency of very heavy cream. Pour into prepared bowls, fold overhang toward the middle and twist gently to seal.

3. Refrigerate for at least 4 hours, until firm, or for up to 5 days. Turn out and use as you would conventional mozzarella.

Recipe Idea

- *Caprese fig salad:* For each serving, slice 1 tomato, 1 green fig and ½ ball mozzarella. Sprinkle with a dash each of olive oil and balsamic vinegar, and a few herbs, and season with salt and pepper.

Spicy Gouda

My own personal veggie variant on the famous Dutch product results in a deliciously scented, mild, firm cheese.

- Immersion blender

3 oz	raw cashews	80 g
1/4 cup	nutritional yeast	60 mL
1 1/2 tsp	onion powder	7 mL
1 tsp	salt	5 mL
1/2 tsp	garlic powder	2 mL
8 tsp	agar agar powder	40 mL
1 2/3 cups	plain soy milk	400 mL
5 tbsp	neutral vegetable oil	75 mL
2 tbsp	white miso	30 mL
2 tsp	freshly squeezed lemon juice	10 mL
1 tsp	tomato paste	5 mL
2 tsp	cumin seeds	10 mL
1 tsp	nigella seeds	5 mL
1/8 tsp	Espelette pepper powder	0.5 mL
	Freshly ground black pepper	
	Additional cumin and nigella seeds	

Serving Suggestions

Serve as is, sliced in sandwiches, with crackers or cut into cubes to accompany drinks.

1. In a tall heatproof cup, using an immersion blender, blend together cashews, yeast, onion powder, salt and garlic powder until fairly finely ground. Set aside.

2. In another tall cup, using the immersion blender, blend together agar agar, soy milk and oil. Add miso, lemon juice and tomato paste; blend until incorporated.

3. Pour soy milk mixture into a medium saucepan and bring to a boil over medium-high heat, stirring constantly with a wooden spoon. Reduce heat and boil, stirring constantly, for 1 to 2 minutes or until slightly thickened. Immediately add to cashew mixture and blend until incorporated.

4. Pour into a large bowl and stir in cumin seeds, nigella seeds, Espelette pepper and black pepper to taste. Pour into flat, shallow dishes or rings and refrigerate for about 2 hours, until set, or for up to 5 days.

5. To decorate, spread cumin seeds and nigella seeds on a shallow plate. Turn out the cheeses and turn them over in the seed mixture, pressing firmly to make them stick.

Feta

This fantastic vegan cheese is probably my favorite recipe in the book. With its unbelievable flavor and perfect texture, it is the perfect way to introduce your friends to plant-based cheeses.

- Immersion blender
- 2¹/₂- to 3-cup (625 to 750 mL) rectangular dish, lined with parchment paper or plastic wrap

7 oz	hulled drained brined lupini beans	200 g
3¹/₂ oz	drained regular lacto-fermented tofu	100 g
1 tsp	salt	5 mL
²/₃ cup	melted odorless coconut oil	150 mL
²/₃ cup	plain soy milk	150 mL
2 tbsp	freshly squeezed lemon juice	30 mL

Tip

The salty taste of the brined lupini beans gives this cheese its feta-like flavor; the lactofermented tofu gives it a very cheesy tang; and the coconut oil holds it together and makes it really melt in the mouth. These products may be hard to find, but don't be tempted to replace them with something else. They can be ordered very easily online.

Serving Suggestions

Serve as you would feta: diced in salads, on bread with olive oil, stuffed into baked summer vegetables, etc.

1. In a tall cup, using an immersion blender, blend together beans, tofu, salt, coconut oil, soy milk and lemon juice for 5 minutes, until as even and smooth as possible.

2. Pour into prepared dish, cover and refrigerate for about 12 hours, until set, or for up to 1 week.

Cashew-Soy Ricotta

This is a multipurpose cheese par excellence, both soft and creamy thanks to the blend of cashews and soy curd. It is ideal for cooking because it holds together well when cooked.

MAKES 4 SERVINGS

- Food processor
- Very fine-mesh sieve, or fine-mesh sieve lined with cheesecloth

5½ oz	raw cashews	150 g
1 tbsp	freshly squeezed lemon juice	15 mL
6 cups	plain soy milk	1.5 L
1½ tsp	nigari powder (magnesium chloride)	7 mL
1½ tsp	salt	7 mL
2 tbsp	water	30 mL

Tip

This cheese uses the same curdling technique that is used to make tofu. Drained soy curd is perfectly edible on its own, just like a lighter ricotta cheese or cottage cheese, but the added cashews make the cheese a little firmer and creamier and contribute an interesting cheesy flavor.

Serving Suggestions

Use along with spinach to stuff cannelloni, add it to turnovers, vegetable tarts or quiches, or simply spread on bread with salt, pepper, fresh herbs and a dash of olive oil.

1. Place cashews in a bowl, cover with water and let soak in a cool place for 4 to 6 hours.

2. Drain cashews and place in food processor. Add lemon juice and process to an even grainy consistency. Set aside.

3. In a deep pot, bring soy milk to a boil over high heat. (Warning: it really froths up when it boils!) Meanwhile, in a small bowl, dissolve nigari and salt in 2 tbsp (30 mL) water. Once the soy milk reaches a boil, remove it from the heat and mix in the nigari mixture. Let curdle for 5 to 10 minutes.

4. Set sieve over a large bowl. Pour curdled soy milk through sieve. Let drain for 15 to 20 minutes.

5. In another large bowl, mix drained soy curd with the processed cashews.

Soft Cheese Log

The classic, flavorsome, multipurpose fresh cheese is as light and creamy as it gets. The mixture of almonds and cashews offers a subtle texture.

- **Immersion blender**

3½ oz	blanched almonds	100 g
3½ oz	raw cashews	100 g
1 tbsp	nutritional yeast	15 mL
	Salt	
2 tsp	freshly squeezed lemon juice	10 mL
½ tsp	white vinegar or white wine vinegar	2 mL
2 tbsp	chopped fresh chives	30 mL
1 tsp	fresh thyme leaves	5 mL
	Freshly ground black pepper	

Serving Suggestions

This cheese is ideal eaten as is, but can also be used to top pizza or toast, or with crumbs in an au gratin topping. It won't melt but will add a little texture and flavor.

1. Place almonds and cashews in separate bowls and cover with water. Let soak in a cool place for 12 hours.
2. Drain almonds and cashews, then transfer to a tall cup. Add yeast, ½ tsp (2 mL) salt, lemon juice and vinegar. Using an immersion blender, blend until fairly smooth.
3. On a sheet of parchment paper, combine chives, thyme and salt and pepper to taste. Spoon the fresh cheese lengthwise in a rough log on the herb mixture. Roll up in paper and smooth into a sausage shape. Twist the ends to seal. Refrigerate for at least 2 hours, until set, or for up to 3 days. Unroll carefully before serving.

Garlic Cancoillotte

This unique vegan version of a classic French cheese has an intriguingly runny consistency when melted.

- Blender
- Immersion blender

1	small clove garlic	1
1½ tbsp	potato starch	22 mL
½ tsp	salt	2 mL
½ tsp	garlic powder	2 mL
1 cup	plain soy milk	250 mL
¼ cup	plain soy yogurt	60 mL
4 tbsp	cashew butter, divided	60 mL
1 tbsp	white miso	15 mL
2 tsp	olive oil	10 mL

Tip

If desired, add more minced garlic to taste after adding the remaining cashew butter.

Serving Suggestions

Ideal with toast or potatoes, or for making an au gratin dish.

1. In blender, combine garlic, potato starch, salt, garlic powder, soy milk, yogurt, 3 tbsp (45 mL) cashew butter, miso and oil; blend until smooth.

2. Transfer to a medium saucepan and cook over medium-high heat, whisking constantly, until the mixture has the consistency of a thick white sauce. Remove from heat and let cool.

3. Blend in the remaining cashew butter using an immersion blender in the pot (or transfer to a tall cup). Use immediately or refrigerate in an airtight jar or container for up to 2 days.

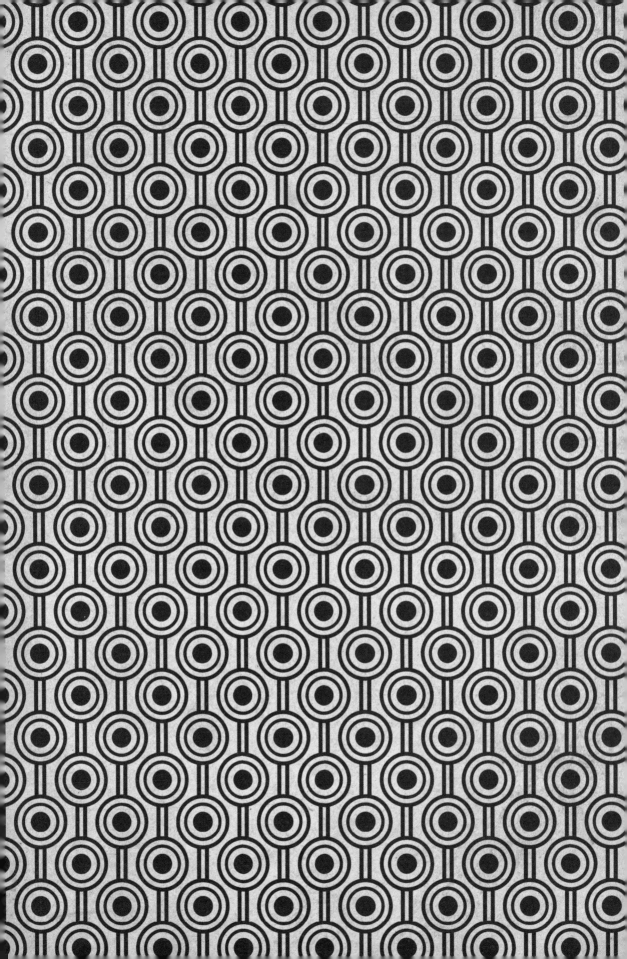

Fermented Cheeses

Creamy Almond Cheese

This simple fresh cheese can be enjoyed on its own or can serve as the base for a multitude of variations. The almost foamy consistency is particularly enjoyable.

MAKES 4 SERVINGS

- **Food processor**
- **2 sterilized 8-oz (250 mL) jars**

4½ oz	blanched almonds	125 g
⅓ cup	rejuvelac (see page 13)	75 mL
	Salt	

Tips

Almonds are high in calcium, so this cheese is a calcium-rich alternative to dairy cheese.

It's best to leave minimal space at the top of the jar when fermenting cheese to avoid mold growth. Check the cheese often while it is fermenting. If the surface starts to discolor or you notice any off odors (though it will develop a sour aroma), discard the cheese and do not consume.

When fermenting the cheese, open the jar each day to let any accumulated gases release from the jar, and taste each day to make sure the flavor isn't becoming too strong.

1. Place almonds in a bowl, cover with water and let soak in a cool place for 12 to 24 hours.

2. Drain off water and place almonds in food processor. Add rejuvelac and process until fairly smooth. Transfer almond cheese to jars, packing and placing plastic wrap on the surface to limit air contact. Seal jars and let ferment at room temperature for 24 to 72 hours or until cheese acquires a slightly fermented flavor.

3. Stir in salt. Use immediately or store in the refrigerator for up to 5 days.

Recipe Ideas

- Bruschetta with cherry tomatoes and basil
- Cheese spread with grilled peppers and lemon
- Soft cheese dip with tapenade
- Savory tartlets with grilled vegetables
- Tomatoes stuffed with almond cheese and herbs
- Almond cheese on toast with figs, hazelnuts and maple syrup

Oven-Baked Almond Cheese Rounds

The texture of almond cheese makes it particularly well suited for forming small round cheeses. Once they are coated in almond meal, the result is quite amazing. Serve hot or cold, as you would a soft baked goat's milk cheese.

- Preheat oven to 350°F (180°C)
- Baking sheet, lined with parchment paper

¼	recipe Creamy Almond Cheese (page 36)	¼
3½ oz	almond meal, divided	100 g

OPTIONAL SEASONING

1 tsp	onion powder	5 mL
¼ tsp	garlic powder	1 mL
	Herbes de Provence	
	Paprika	
	Freshly ground black pepper	
	Salt	

Serving Suggestions

Serve on toast, in chunks in a salad, in sandwiches, with figs, black cherry jam, chutney or olives, in savory tarts or on pizzas.

1. In a bowl, combine almond cheese with about 3 oz (80 g) almond meal. If desired, add onion powder, garlic powder and herbes de Provence, paprika, pepper and salt to taste.

2. Shape into 6 small balls, then roll the balls in the remaining almond meal. Flatten them gently between your hands and shape them into small disks. Place on prepared baking sheet.

3. Bake in preheated oven for 5 to 10 minutes or until warmed through. Serve hot or cold.

Cashew Cheese

This classic vegan cheese has a texture as creamy as they come, and it tastes delicious — what I call a must-have!

- Immersion blender
- Sterilized pint (500 mL) jar

4¹⁄₂ oz	raw cashews	125 g
7 tbsp	rejuvelac (see page 13)	100 mL
¹⁄₂ tsp	salt	2 mL
2 tsp	nutritional yeast	10 mL

Tips

It's best to leave minimal space at the top of the jar when fermenting cheese to avoid mold growth. Check the cheese often while it is fermenting. If the surface starts to discolor or you notice any off odors (though it will develop a sour aroma), discard the cheese and do not consume.

When fermenting the cheese, open the jar each day to let any accumulated gases release from the jar, and taste each day to make sure the flavor isn't becoming too strong. In colder temperatures, fermentation can take over 48 hours. In that case, check every 12 hours whether it is sufficiently fermented.

Serving Suggestions

Serve with sun-dried tomatoes and oregano; herbes de Provence and olive oil; tarragon; dill and smoked paprika; walnuts — the options are endless.

1. Place cashews in a bowl, cover with water and let soak in a cool place for 12 hours.

2. Drain off water and transfer cashews to a tall cup. Add rejuvelac and, using an immersion blender, blend until smooth. Transfer cashew cheese to jar, seal jar and let ferment at room temperature for about 48 hours or until cheese acquires a slightly fermented flavor.

3. Stir in salt and yeast, then place in a cool place.

Recipe Ideas

- Stuffed zucchini
- Cannelloni with cashew cheese and fried chard
- Cheese dip
- Grilled eggplant

Italian-Style Cheese Cakes

This amazing recipe turns cashews into delicious little cheese cakes that are ideal for brunch or with drinks. Thanks to the polenta, the recipe is gluten-free.

MAKES 2 MINI CAKES, 2 TO 4 SERVINGS

- Food processor
- Sterilized half-pint (250 mL) jar
- Two mini loaf pans, lined with parchment paper

3½ oz	raw cashews	100 g
⅓ cup	rejuvelac (see page 13)	75 mL
4	sun-dried tomatoes, thinly sliced	4
2 tbsp	precooked polenta	30 mL
5 tsp	nutritional yeast	25 mL
2 tsp	onion powder	10 mL
½ tsp	garlic powder	2 mL
¼ tsp	Espelette pepper powder	1 mL
¼ tsp	salt	1 mL
1 tbsp	nutritional yeast	15 mL

Tip

It's best to leave minimal space at the top of the jar when fermenting cheese to avoid mold growth. Check the cheese often while it is fermenting. If the surface starts to discolor or you notice any off odors (though it will develop a sour aroma), discard the cheese and do not consume.

Serving Suggestions

Perfect with arugula salad or on small skewers with green olives and cherry tomatoes.

1. Place cashews in a bowl, cover with water and let soak in a cool place for 4 to 12 hours.

2. Drain off water and place cashews in food processor. Add rejuvelac and process until smooth. Transfer cashew cheese to jar, seal jar and let ferment at room temperature for about 48 hours or until cheese acquires a slightly fermented flavor.

3. Preheat oven to 350°F (180°C).

4. Transfer fermented cashew cheese to a medium bowl. Stir in sun-dried tomatoes, polenta, 5 tsp (25 mL) yeast, onion powder, garlic powder, Espelette pepper and salt until well combined. Pack into prepared loaf pans.

5. Bake for 15 minutes or until set. Turn out and sprinkle with 1 tbsp (15 mL) yeast. Serve slightly warm or cold, cut into slices.

Sauerkraut Cheese

The originality of this cheese lies in the use of sauerkraut juice to soak the cashews. Oven-drying the cheese makes it firm on the outside while still very soft in the center.

MAKES 4 SERVINGS

- High-powered blender
- 3-inch (7.5 cm) metal ring (such as a springform pan ring)
- Baking sheet, lined with parchment paper

3½ oz	raw cashews	100 g
1 cup	sauerkraut juice	250 mL
2 tbsp	cashew butter	30 mL
1 tbsp	nutritional yeast	15 mL
½ tsp	salt	2 mL
3 tbsp	sauerkraut juice	45 mL

Tip

This cheese, once cooled, can be stored in an airtight container in the refrigerator for up to 5 days.

1. In a bowl, combine cashews and 1 cup (250 mL) sauerkraut juice. Let soak overnight.
2. Preheat oven to 200°F (100°C).
3. Drain off juice and transfer cashews to the blender. Add cashew butter, yeast, salt and 3 tbsp (45 mL) sauerkraut juice; blend until smooth.
4. Place metal ring on prepared baking sheet. Pack cheese tightly into the ring.
5. Bake for 20 to 30 minutes or until top of cheese is dry, firm and golden. Let cool completely on a plate, then run a knife along the inside of the ring and carefully turn out cheese.

Kombucha Cheese

Kombucha, a sparkling drink revered for its probiotic and detoxification properties, lends its characteristic tang to this unique cheese.

MAKES 4 SERVINGS

- Immersion blender
- Two 3-inch (7.5 cm) metal rings (such as springform pan rings) or two lightly greased dishes
- Baking sheet, lined with parchment paper (optional)

2³/₄ oz	raw cashews	75 g
1¹/₄ cups	kombucha, divided	300 mL
2 tbsp	nutritional yeast	30 mL
4 tsp	agar agar powder	20 mL
1 tbsp	tapioca starch	15 mL
1 tsp	salt	5 mL
1 tsp	Dijon mustard	5 mL
¹/₃ cup	melted odorless virgin coconut oil	75 mL

Tip

Kombucha is readily available at organic grocers, which is very handy when you are unable to make it yourself.

Variations

For a milder cheese, use kefir in place of the kombucha.

For scrumptious variety, add minced garlic, onion powder, herbs, spices, grilled peppers, dried tomatoes, figs — or whatever you fancy — to this basic recipe.

1. Place cashews in a bowl, cover with water and let soak in a cool place for 6 to 12 hours.

2. Drain off water and transfer cashews to a tall cup. Add two-thirds of the kombucha and, using an immersion blender, blend until smooth.

3. In a small saucepan, whisk together yeast, agar agar, tapioca starch, salt, mustard, coconut oil and the remaining kombucha. Gradually stir in cashew mixture. Cook, whisking constantly, over medium-high heat for 4 to 5 minutes or until slightly thickened. (Take care not to cook for too long, or the oil will separate.)

4. If using rings, place them on the prepared baking sheet. Pour kombucha cheese mixture into rings or prepared dishes. Refrigerate for 2 to 3 hours or until set. Store in an airtight container in the refrigerator for up to 2 weeks.

Tofu Cheese with Two Peppers

This *fromage frais* recipe is reminiscent of Boursin-type flavored cheese. Here, the lactofermented tofu adds the fresh cheese taste and the cashews lend creaminess.

MAKES 4 SERVINGS

- Mortar and pestle
- Food processor
- Small flat-bottomed bowl or metal ring, lined with plastic wrap

1/2 cup	raw cashews	125 mL
1/2 tsp	black peppercorns	2 mL
1/2 tsp	pink peppercorns	2 mL
7 oz	drained lactofermented tofu marinated in tamari, crumbled	200 g
1/2 tsp	salt	2 mL
1/4 tsp	garlic powder	1 mL
1/4 cup	water	60 mL
1 1/2 tsp	freshly squeezed lemon juice	7 mL

GARNISH

2 tsp	black peppercorns	10 mL
2 tsp	pink peppercorns	10 mL

Tip

Pink peppercorns are the berries of the Brazilian pepper (*Schinus terebinthifolius*), so, strictly speaking, they do not belong in the pepper family at all. Since they are toxic in high doses, it is recommended to avoid overindulging. But rest assured that a portion or two of this delicious cheese won't do you any harm.

1. Place cashews in a bowl, cover with water and let soak for 2 hours.

2. Using the mortar and pestle, grind black and pink peppercorns.

3. Drain water from cashews and place cashews in food processor. Add tofu, ground peppercorns, salt, garlic powder, water and lemon juice; process to a thick, even consistency.

4. Pack cheese tightly into prepared bowl or ring on a baking sheet. Refrigerate for 30 minutes then turn out onto a plate.

5. *Garnish:* Grind the black and pink peppercorns and sprinkle over the outside of the cheese.

6. Serve immediately or store, covered, in the refrigerator. Best eaten within 48 hours.

Variation

For a smoother version to use as a spread (or to cook with), add 1 to 2 tbsp (15 to 30 mL) more water in step 3, then transfer the cheese to a small bowl or jar after blending. Omit the garnish or sprinkle it on top of the bowl before serving.

Tofu Misozuke

This traditional recipe from Fukuoka, Japan, is often compared with both cheese and foie gras. The longer you let it ferment, the more fragrant and creamy it becomes. Although it can be hard to find, even in Japan, it is very easy to make at home.

MAKES 4 TO 8 SERVINGS

- **Cheesecloth**

8 oz	firm tofu, cut into 2 slabs	250 g
2 tbsp	granulated sugar	30 mL
7 oz	white miso	200 g
2 tbsp	sake	30 mL

Tips

The optimum fermentation time for a good tofu misozuke is 2 months. But if you can't wait that long, the tofu will still have a delightful flavor and texture after 1 week; it just won't melt in your mouth quite so much.

For a stronger flavor, mix some brown miso in with the white miso — the more brown miso, the stronger the flavor will be.

If any mold appears on the tofu, throw it away and start over.

1. Roll each slab of tofu in paper towels and place a weight (such as a plate) over it; let drain for 1 hour. Remove paper towels and wrap tofu in cheesecloth. Line an airtight container with paper towels and place tofu inside.

2. In a bowl, combine sugar, miso and sake. Spread over tofu. Cover and refrigerate for at least 1 week or for up to 2 months, changing the paper towels as needed to prevent it from becoming too moist.

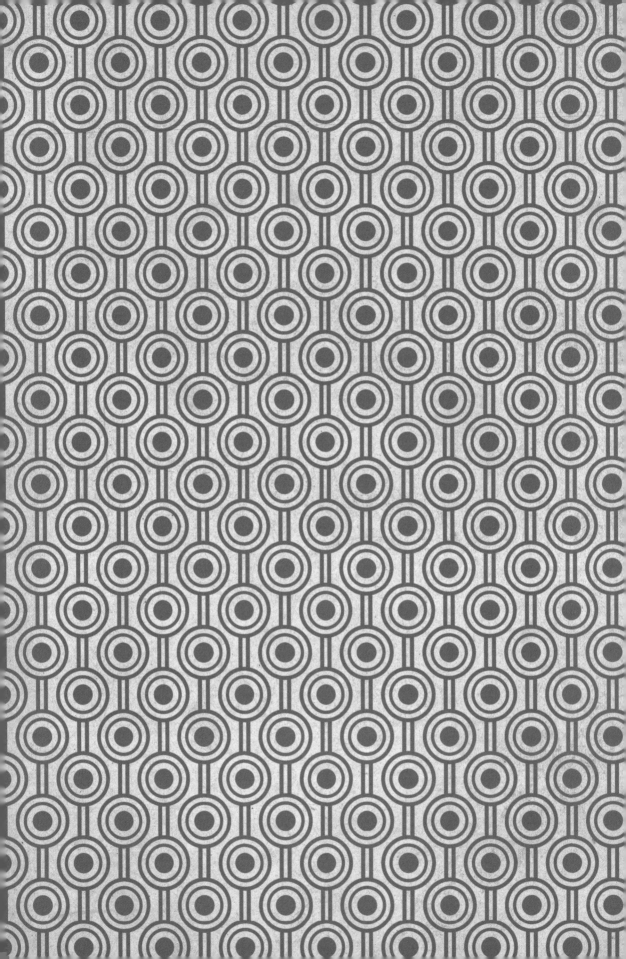

Specialty Cheeses

Cheese with Olives and Rosemary

There is a touch of Provence about this drained soft cheese, which is very easy to prepare and requires only a few ingredients.

MAKES 2 TO 4 SERVINGS

- Immersion blender
- Fine-mesh sieve, lined with cheesecloth

2$\frac{3}{4}$ oz	raw cashews	75 g
7 oz	plain soy yogurt	200 g
1 tbsp	freshly squeezed lemon juice	15 mL
$\frac{1}{2}$ tsp	salt	2 mL
3 tbsp	chopped pitted green olives	45 mL
	Chopped fresh rosemary	
	Freshly ground black pepper	

1. Place cashews in a bowl, cover with water and let soak in a cool place for 4 to 12 hours.

2. Drain off water and transfer cashews to a tall cup. Add yogurt and, using an immersion blender, blend until smooth. Add lemon juice and salt; pulse until blended.

3. Set prepared sieve over a large bowl. Pour cashew mixture into cheesecloth. Fold the edges of the cheesecloth and tie it shut. Let drain for 6 to 12 hours, until thickened. Discard liquid.

4. Transfer drained cashew cheese to a bowl and stir in olives, and rosemary and pepper to taste. Serve immediately or cover and refrigerate for up to 3 days.

Three-Seed Cheese with Pine Nuts

This richly textured cheese melts in the mouth, and it provides omega-3s thanks to the flax seeds and hemp seeds.

- Immersion blender

3½ oz	drained lactofermented tofu, crumbled	100 g
2½ oz	hulled drained brined lupini beans	70 g
1 oz	pine nuts	30 g
1 tbsp	nutritional yeast	15 mL
2 tsp	salt	10 mL
2 tsp	onion powder	10 mL
½ tsp	garlic powder	2 mL
2 tbsp	water	30 mL
2 tbsp	cashew butter	30 mL
1 tbsp	tahini	15 mL
2 tsp	freshly squeezed lemon juice	10 mL
⅔ cup	plain soy milk	150 mL
4 tsp	agar agar powder	20 mL
4 tsp	hulled hemp seed hearts	20 mL
2 tsp	flax seeds	10 mL
2 tsp	sesame seeds	10 mL
	Additional flax seeds and sesame seeds	

1. In a tall cup, combine tofu, lupini beans, pine nuts, yeast, salt, onion powder, garlic powder, water, cashew butter, tahini and lemon juice. Using an immersion blender, purée into a thick, grainy paste. Set aside.

2. In a small saucepan, combine soy milk and agar agar. Bring to a boil over medium-high heat, stirring constantly. Boil, stirring, for 2 minutes or until slightly thickened.

3. Add soy milk mixture to tofu mixture. Stir in hemp seeds, flax seeds and sesame seeds until evenly blended.

4. Shape into small balls, flat rounds, slabs or logs and roll in a mixture of flax seeds and sesame seeds. Store in an airtight container in the refrigerator for up to 5 days.

Cheese with Figs and Walnuts

The combination of cashew, tempeh and lactofermented tofu gives an interesting flavor to this mild but characterful cheese — an original combination but already almost a classic, to be made with green figs in summer or with black figs in the fall.

MAKES 4 SERVINGS

- Immersion blender
- Flat-bottomed bowl or metal ring, lined with plastic wrap

3½ oz	raw cashews	100 g
5½ oz	drained lactofermented tofu marinated in tamari, crumbled	150 g
1¾ oz	plain tempeh, crumbled	50 g
1 tbsp	onion powder	15 mL
1 tsp	salt	5 mL
4½ tbsp	melted odorless coconut oil	70 mL
3 tbsp	freshly squeezed lemon juice	45 mL
1 tbsp	white miso	15 mL
2½ tbsp	finely chopped walnuts	37 mL
2	fresh figs, finely chopped	2
	Fresh figs, cut into wedges (optional)	

Serving Suggestions

Perfect on toasted whole wheat bread, with a few slices of fried figs and a salad of lamb's lettuce, apple, grapes, walnut oil and balsamic vinegar.

1. Place cashews in a bowl, cover with water and let soak in a cool place for 4 to 12 hours.

2. Drain off water and transfer cashews to a tall cup. Add tofu, tempeh, onion powder, salt, coconut oil, lemon juice and miso; using an immersion blender, blend until smooth. Add walnuts and figs, then gently mix with a fork.

3. Pack cheese tightly into prepared bowl or ring on a baking sheet. Refrigerate for 30 minutes or until set, then turn out onto a plate.

4. Serve immediately or store, covered, in the refrigerator for up to 3 days. Garnish with fig wedges just before serving, if desired.

Tempeh Pavé

Tempeh is made from fermented cooked soybeans that are formed into a cheese-like mold. So a cheese based on this product just makes sense.

MAKES 1 BLOCK, 4 TO 8 SERVINGS

- Immersion blender
- 2-cup (500 mL) shallow square or rectangle dish, lined with plastic wrap
- Electric food dehydrator or oven with dehydrator function

4¹/₂ oz	plain tempeh, crumbled	125 g
	Nutritional yeast	
1 tbsp	onion powder	15 mL
	Salt	
³/₄ cup + 2 tbsp	plain soy milk, divided	200 mL
3 tbsp	neutral vegetable oil	45 mL
2 tbsp	cashew butter	30 mL
1 tbsp	white miso	15 mL
2 tsp	freshly squeezed lemon juice	10 mL
4 tsp	agar agar powder	20 mL

1. In a tall cup, combine tempeh, 2 tbsp (30 mL) yeast, onion powder, ¹/₂ tsp (2 mL) salt, 6 tbsp (90 mL) soy milk, oil, cashew butter, miso and lemon juice. Using an immersion blender, blend until smooth. Set aside.

2. In a small saucepan, combine agar agar and the remaining soy milk; bring to a boil over medium-high heat, stirring constantly. Boil, stirring, for about 2 minutes or until thickened to a consistency midway between cream and jelly.

3. Add soy milk mixture to tempeh mixture and blend well. Add salt and yeast to taste, pulsing to combine. Pour into prepared dish. Cover and refrigerate for about 2 hours or until set.

4. Turn out of dish onto a piece of parchment paper, removing plastic. Dehydrate at 100°F (40°C) for 5 hours, until very firm and thoroughly dry on the outside. Let cool completely.

5. Serve immediately or wrap in parchment paper, then place in an airtight container or storage bag and refrigerate for up to 1 week.

Kimcheese

If you are unfamiliar with kimchi, you may think it's a rather crazy idea to include this Korean fermented vegetable dish in cheese. But try it once and you'll understand: when you're mad about kimchi, you want kimchi with everything!

MAKES 6 TO 8 SERVINGS

- Immersion blender
- Flat-bottomed bowl or metal ring, lined with plastic wrap

7 oz	raw cashews	200 g
2³/₄ oz	drained kimchi	75 g
1 tbsp	juice drained from kimchi	15 mL
¹/₂ tsp	garlic powder	2 mL
¹/₂ tsp	onion powder	2 mL
¹/₂ tsp	salt	2 mL
7 tbsp	melted odorless coconut oil	100 mL
1¹/₂ tbsp	freshly squeezed lemon juice	22 mL
1 tbsp	white miso	15 mL

1. Place cashews in a bowl, cover with water and let soak in a cool place for 4 to 12 hours.
2. Drain off water and transfer cashews to a tall cup. Add kimchi, kimchi juice, garlic powder, onion powder, salt, coconut oil, lemon juice and miso; using an immersion blender, blend until smooth.
3. Pack cheese tightly into prepared bowl or ring on a baking sheet. Refrigerate for 6 minutes or until set, then turn out onto a plate.
4. Serve immediately or store, covered, in the refrigerator for up to 3 days.

Hummus Cheese Dip

While a hummus-cheese combination may at first strike you as odd, you are sure to love this amazingly cheesy dip that you can rustle up in just a few minutes.

- Immersion blender or food processor

8½ oz	cooked chickpeas	250 g
1 to 2	cloves garlic	1 to 2
4 tsp	nutritional yeast	20 mL
¼ tsp	salt	1 mL
¼ cup	cashew butter	60 mL
2 tbsp	freshly squeezed lemon juice	30 mL
1 tbsp	olive oil	15 mL
¼ cup	water (approx.)	60 mL

Serving Suggestions

Serve as a dip with a dash of olive oil and a pinch of za'atar; with Lebanese bread browned in the oven, bread sticks or raw or fried cauliflower; as a spread for sandwiches or wraps; as a garnish for savory tartlets; or as a topping for cooked pizza.

1. In a tall cup (if using an immersion blender) or in food processor, combine chickpeas, garlic to taste, yeast, salt, cashew butter, lemon juice and oil; process to a smooth, creamy, thick consistency. Add just enough water, 1 tbsp (15 mL) at a time, until the desired consistency is reached. Serve immediately or refrigerate in an airtight container for up to 3 days.

Recipe Ideas

- Pastry turnovers with sautéed spinach
- Creamy quesadillas
- Stuffed zucchini

Creamy Shallot and Chive Cheese Spread

Here we have a variation on the "cashews and lactofermented tofu" theme, offering an ultra-creamy cheese spread that you can lay on as thick as you like!

- **Immersion blender**

3 oz	raw cashews	85 g
3½ oz	drained lactofermented tofu, crumbled	100 g
½ tsp	salt	2 mL
2 tbsp	water	30 mL
1½ tbsp	freshly squeezed lemon juice	22 mL
1 tbsp	minced shallot	15 mL
1 tbsp	chopped fresh chives	15 mL

Tip

The base for this cheese works well with many other flavors; instead of the shallots and chives, try pesto, pepper and mint, dill and lemon, curry and cumin seeds, hazelnuts and dried fruit, garlic and fresh thyme, etc.

Serving Suggestions

Add to lasagna or to liven up soup, or use to make grilled cheese and eggplant sandwiches.

1. Place cashews in a bowl, cover with water and let soak in a cool place for 4 to 12 hours.

2. Drain off water and transfer cashews to a tall cup. Add tofu, salt, water and lemon juice; using an immersion blender, blend until smooth. Stir in shallot and chives with a fork.

3. Cover and refrigerate for about 30 minutes, until chilled, or for up to 3 days.

Vegan Fondue with White Wine

It would be such a pity to do without this classic of French cuisine when the vegan version is so easy and delicious. Cashew butter gives this recipe its inimitable smoothness.

MAKES 4 TO 6 SERVINGS

- Blender
- Fondue pot, small slow cooker or warmed dish

2 cups	plain soy milk	500 mL
2 tbsp	potato starch	30 mL
2 tbsp	nutritional yeast	30 mL
1 tsp	salt	5 mL
1 tsp	garlic powder	5 mL
2/3 cup	vegan white wine	150 mL
9 tbsp	cashew butter	135 mL
1/4 cup	neutral vegetable oil (not coconut oil)	60 mL
	Bread pieces, potato chunks, vegan charcuterie, etc.	

Serving Suggestions

Use to top baked potatoes or to make a very cool cauliflower au gratin.

1. In blender, combine soy milk, potato starch, yeast, salt, garlic powder, wine, cashew butter and oil; blend until smooth.

2. Transfer to a medium saucepan and cook over medium-high heat, stirring constantly, for about 5 minutes or until mixture thickens and becomes nice and creamy (some of the alcohol from the wine will evaporate as it cooks).

3. Transfer to fondue pot set over burner, slow cooker set on warm or warmed dish and serve with pieces of bread, potatoes and vegan charcuterie.

Nacho Cheese Sauce

Use this cheddar sauce as a dip or to create an au gratin dish for a moment of sheer delight!

MAKES 4 TO 6 SERVINGS

- **Blender**

7 oz	Cheddar with Roasted Red Pepper (page 20), chopped	200 g
1$\frac{1}{2}$ cups	plain soy milk	350 mL
1$\frac{1}{2}$ tbsp	cornstarch	22 mL
3 tbsp	neutral vegetable oil	45 mL
	Hot pepper sauce	
	Salt	
	Jalapeño peppers or mild green chile peppers, thinly sliced or chopped	

Tip

If you let the sauce cool, you will need to mix it a little with an immersion blender before serving, as it tends to set.

Serving Suggestions

Use as a dip with corn chips, to garnish tortillas, for enchiladas or burritos au gratin or, of course, for nachos!

1. In blender, combine cheddar, soy milk, cornstarch and oil; blend until fairly smooth. Season to taste with hot pepper sauce and salt.
2. Transfer to a small saucepan and cook over medium-high heat, stirring constantly, for about 5 minutes or until thickened. Serve with sliced jalapeños or, if you prefer, add chopped jalapeños directly to the sauce.

PART 2

Vegan
Ice Cream

The Different Types of Ice Cream

Ah, ice cream . . . Just sinking your spoon into it makes you feel like you're on vacation. Whether it's a simple cone on a summer's day or a festive dessert to crown a holiday meal, ice cream is associated with happy times shared with loved ones. Ice cream is an invitation to savor the moment and focus on the pure pleasure of tasting as it melts in your mouth.

If you're vegan, enjoying a cone or dish of ice cream can be a challenge. Luckily, you can find sorbets at ice cream shops, and there are more varieties of non-dairy ice cream available than ever before. Finding ice cream logs or other frozen desserts that are 100% organic is a little more complicated. Making your own at home is an economical, healthy and surprisingly easy solution.

Among these 25 fabulous frosty recipes you'll find sorbets, ice cream, ice pops and cones, along with frozen desserts designed to be shared. Enjoying vegan ice cream should not be an obstacle course but an occasion to savor the moment and experience the pleasure of a decadent and delicious dessert.

Ice Cream

Ice cream is what will interest us most in this book, because it can be difficult to find vegan ice cream in ice cream shops or in stores (although this is gradually changing). As its name suggests, ice cream has a creamy texture and can be flavored with any ingredients you desire. Caramel bits, cookie pieces and nuts of all kinds are often included.

Soft-Serve Ice Cream

Soft-serve ice cream is served out of a refrigerated machine that maintains the product at a temperature of about 21°F (−6°C) to keep it soft, while a freezer can chill to about 0°F (−18°C).

Gelato

Gelato is lighter than ice cream. Like soft-serve ice cream, it is served at a temperature of about 21°F (−6°C).

Frozen Yogurt

"Froyo" is simply frozen yogurt to which coulis, fresh fruit or toppings like sprinkles, chocolate chips or nuts have been added. Ice cream shops serve up this product with the same machines that are used for Italian-style gelato, so it is fairly soft.

Sorbet

Sorbet is usually made from fruit, water and sugar. If eggs or dairy products figure in the recipe, it is no longer a sorbet. Note that there are a few exceptions: vegetable, herbal, flower or cocoa sorbets are not fruit-based, but still do not contain any ingredients of animal origin. Sorbet is, therefore, in theory always vegan. It is still a good idea to inquire at the ice cream shop and check the ingredients in all products. Egg whites, gelatin and milk occasionally slip into commercially prepared sorbet.

Sherbet

A sherbet is a sorbet to which milk, eggs or cream have been added, without turning it into ice cream, and is therefore richer than sorbet.

Ice Pops

Sold just about everywhere in the world and popular with children because of their dazzling colors and candy (lemon, orange, strawberry) or cola flavors, water-based ice pops consist of water, sugar and flavorings, or water and syrup. They are often molded on a stick. It is very easy to make them at home. For a healthier version, you can mix a homemade fruit coulis or sauce with water, or simply freeze fruit juice.

Equipment

Making ice cream at home calls for a certain amount of equipment. Some utensils are indispensable, others optional. It's for you to decide what will be the most useful.

Preparing Ice Cream

Basic pastry-making equipment is a must. This includes a whisk, metal bowls, a small and a large saucepan, a rubber spatula and metal ring molds. As for electrical appliances, you will need a blender. Failing that, you will need an immersion blender and perhaps an electric mixer. A pastry bag fitted with a large star tip is handy for serving soft-serve ice cream.

Storing Ice Cream

Forget glass and ceramic containers. These may crack as your ice cream sets and expands. Instead, use containers made of stainless steel, enameled metal or BPA-free plastic that come with a lid or that can be sealed with plastic wrap to make them airtight. You will need a loaf pan for frozen dessert logs or Neapolitan-style desserts. Small molds are also handy.

Ice Cream Maker: Freezer Bowl Model

I wish I could say you can do just fine without an ice cream maker, but I can't. For sorbet and ice cream, an ice cream maker is pretty much indispensable. Without one, you have to mix your ice cream every 45 minutes or every hour with an immersion blender. It's a long process and requires being available for half a day. Without an ice cream maker,

your ice cream will be less smooth and more granular.

You can find inexpensive models with a bowl you freeze ahead of time and an electric motor (or a hand-crank) to churn the ice cream. These work very well and are sufficient for non-intensive use. The inconvenience of finding a place to store it is often what makes someone hesitate to invest in this appliance. Also available are ice cream attachments for stand mixers.

Note that ice cream makers that need to be put in the freezer have generally been abandoned in favor of models that come with a separate chilling bowl that goes in the freezer.

Ice Cream Maker: Compressor Model

Unlike the freezer bowl model, which includes a chilling bowl to place in the freezer before transferring it back to the ice cream maker to make the ice cream, this machine has its own refrigeration system and chills the ice cream while it's churning. It's larger and more expensive, but allows you to make one batch of ice cream after another. It is designed for intensive use and for professionals.

Ice Pop Molds

These are found everywhere, in all shapes and every price range. They are usually made of durable plastic (there are stainless steel models for professionals) and often come with covers or lids with sticks built in. My advice: check where the plastic molds come from and ensure they are BPA-free. You can also improvise by using plastic liqueur-style glasses instead of molds.

Key Ingredients

Vegan ice cream contains no cream or milk of animal origin, but ample use is made of vegan creams and milks, as well as cashew and other nut butters.

Soy Cream

This is the cream I use the most, because its texture and composition are ideal. It has a more neutral flavor than other vegan creams. (Oat cream, for example, is fine for a curry but not for ice cream.) You can replace soy cream with almond cream or rice cream if you are soy intolerant, but their composition and taste will change the texture and flavor of the ice cream.

Vegan Milks

I prefer almond milk for its smoothness and color. It is very white compared to some brands of soy milk, which can be fairly yellow or dark. Once almond milk is frozen, its flavor is neutral. And an economic advantage: this milk can be made very easily at home, without any specific equipment. Use plain, unsweetened non-dairy milks in these recipes.

Coconut Milk

Coconut milk is the magic ingredient for making vegan ice cream quickly and easily. The recipes in this book use canned coconut milk, not the cartons of coconut milk beverage (which is a different formula). Just sweeten the coconut milk and let it set in the ice cream maker for rich and delicious ice cream. I leave it to you to come up with your own tasty blends of tropical fruit, chocolate or caramel!

Plain Soy Yogurt

This is a must for making frozen yogurt, of course, but that's not all! It can be added to vegan ice cream to lighten it and add a slightly tart note. It is also your ally in ice pop recipes. Simply mix it with fresh fruit and a little sugar, then pop it in the freezer.

Cashews

Fans of vegan cuisine know this trick: cashews soaked and blended with a liquid form a thick, rich cream that is close to mascarpone. Used for vegan cheeses and raw desserts, it is also very popular in ultra-healthy homemade ice cream recipes.

Nut Butters

Cashew butter and almond butter are fats that add smoothness and creaminess to ice cream. "Gourmet" nut butters, such as hazelnut butter (the roasted variety is tastier) and pistachio butter, add wonderful flavor to ice cream recipes.

Sugar

For recipes that call for sugar, I use light cane sugar, which has a more neutral flavor than raw cane sugar. When possible, I use agave syrup or rice syrup instead.

Homemade Cones

Making your own ice cream is fun, economical and creative. When I was thinking about the recipes in this book, it seemed obvious to me that I should provide you with a recipe to make your own cones. Commercial vegan cones are fairly easy to find, but they are rarely organic. So here is my recipe for cones that are crispy and waffle-textured. You'll need a special waffle cone waffle maker or pizzelle maker as well as a cone roller to make the cones.

MAKES ABOUT 8 CONES

- Preheat waffle cone maker to medium
- Cone roller

1 cup	all-purpose flour	250 mL
1 tbsp	cornstarch	15 mL
5 tbsp	neutral vegetable oil	75 mL
2 tbsp	cashew butter	30 mL
1/4 cup	light cane sugar	60 mL
1/4 tsp	salt	1 mL
1 tsp	vanilla extract	5 mL
1 tsp	orange blossom extract (optional)	5 mL
1 cup	almond milk	250 mL
	Neutral vegetable oil	

Tips

To seal cones completely (there is often a little hole at the tip) and prevent ice cream from dripping out, you can pour a little melted chocolate over the tip (or dip the tip of the cone in melted chocolate) and let it harden in the refrigerator.

If you have difficulty making your cones, here are a few hints to help you identify the cause: the waffle maker is not sufficiently greased; the waffle maker is too hot or not hot enough; you have opened the waffle maker before the waffle is completely cooked (which may cause the waffle to break apart).

1. In a medium bowl, sift together flour and cornstarch.

2. In a large bowl, whisk together oil and cashew butter. Add sugar, salt, vanilla and orange blossom extract (if using); whisk to combine. Gradually stir in almond milk, then stir in flour mixture.

3. Oil the waffle maker, then pour about half a ladleful of batter into the center and close the waffle maker. Wait 2 to 3 minutes (or follow the directions that come with the appliance), then open the waffle maker and remove the waffle with a heatproof spatula. Lay the waffle on a clean, lint-free tea towel folded into quarters, then immediately roll it around the cone roller, using the towel to help shape the waffle. Do not touch the waffle directly, as it is very hot. Let cool, then store in an airtight container at room temperature for up to 5 days. Repeat with the remaining batter.

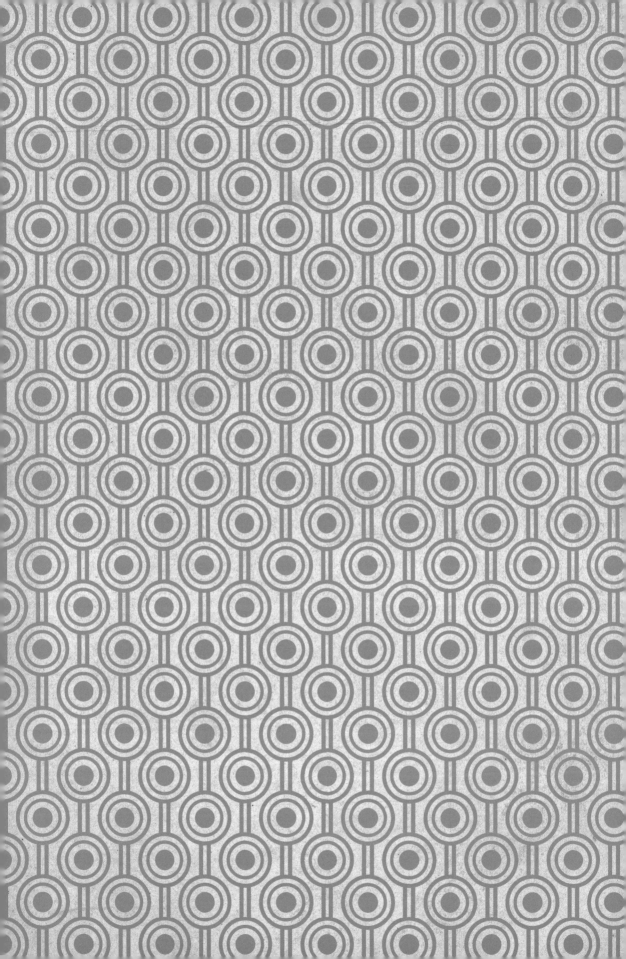

Ice Cream and Sorbet

Vanilla Ice Cream

The quintessential vanilla ice cream. After testing several recipes, including French-style ice cream with a custard base, I'm sold on this astonishingly simple version. I've made it time and time again, and it always turns out beautifully. The secret of really flavorful vanilla ice cream lies in the quality of the vanilla. Always use vanilla bean pods and not extract.

MAKES 4 TO 6 SERVINGS

- **Ice cream maker**

$1^2/_3$ cups	soy cream	400 mL
7 tbsp	rice cream for cooking	100 mL
5 tbsp	light cane sugar	75 mL
	Seeds from $1^1/_2$ vanilla bean pods	

Tips

You can add anything to this basic recipe: chocolate chips, cookie pieces, bits of salted caramel, etc.

For a decadent topping, try this quick chocolate-caramel sauce: Mix the same quantity of melted dark chocolate and caramel sundae topping with a few spoonfuls of warm water. Top your ice cream with this warm sauce and caramelized almonds.

1. In a saucepan, over medium heat, whisk together soy cream, rice cream, sugar and vanilla seeds until sugar is dissolved. Let cool.
2. Churn in ice cream maker according to manufacturer's directions.
3. Transfer to an airtight container and freeze for at least 5 hours. Remove ice cream from freezer about 20 minutes before serving to give it time to soften.

Coconut Mint Stracciatella

This ultra-creamy ice cream with the subtle flavor of coconut, thin shavings of crunchy chocolate and finely chopped mint strikes the perfect balance between refinement and indulgence.

MAKES 6 SERVINGS

- **Ice cream maker**

1	can (14 oz/400 mL) coconut milk	1
1²/₃ cups	rice cream for cooking	400 mL
5 tbsp	light cane sugar	75 mL
1³/₄ oz	dark chocolate (70% cocoa)	50 g
¹/₄ cup	finely chopped fresh mint leaves	60 mL

Variations

For marbled ice cream, omit the chocolate and mint and add mango coulis, swirling it into just-frozen ice cream as you transfer it to the container.

To make a rich and flavorful vanilla ice cream, omit the chocolate and mint and add ¹/₂ tsp (2 mL) vanilla bean powder.

1. In a saucepan, over medium heat, stir coconut milk, rice cream and sugar until sugar is dissolved and mixture is smooth. Let cool.

2. Churn in ice cream maker according to manufacturer's directions.

3. Use a vegetable peeler to reduce chocolate to thin shavings.

4. When the ice cream is just frozen, add chocolate shavings and chopped mint. Let ice cream maker churn a few rotations to blend in chocolate and mint.

5. Transfer to an airtight container and freeze for at least 5 hours. Remove from freezer about 20 minutes before serving to allow ice cream to soften slightly.

Pistachio Ice Cream

Pistachio ice cream on a cone is one of my tastiest childhood memories. I couldn't resist revisiting this recipe as an entirely vegan and organic version. Unlike commercial ice cream, this ice cream contains real whole pistachios, as well as pistachio nut butter for additional smoothness.

MAKES 4 TO 6 SERVINGS

- **Blender**
- **Ice cream maker**

2 cups	plain soy milk	450 mL
3/4 cup + 2 tbsp	soy cream	200 mL
3 tbsp	pistachio nut butter	45 mL
7 tbsp	light cane sugar	100 mL
1/4 cup	unsalted pistachios, coarsely chopped	60 mL

Tips

To make cones, dip the edges of a cone in melted chocolate and sprinkle with chopped pistachios. Let harden in refrigerator. Fill with pistachio ice cream and serve immediately, or wrap in parchment paper, fold paper over the top and hold it in place with adhesive tape. Store in freezer. Now you have ready-to-eat cones!

Real pistachios do not turn ice cream the bright green you see in commercial ice cream, which contains artificial colors. If you want a beautiful green shade, mix in a small handful of spinach leaves with the milk and cream in step 1. The spinach will add color and plenty of minerals and vitamins, but no flavor. You can also add two spoonfuls of matcha green tea powder or wheat grass powder for a less neutral, slightly herbaceous flavor. These ingredients provide additional nutritional benefits.

1. In blender, combine soy milk, soy cream and pistachio nut butter; blend until smooth.
2. In a saucepan, over medium heat, stir soy mixture and sugar until sugar is dissolved. Let cool, then transfer to a bowl and refrigerate until chilled.
3. Churn in ice cream maker according to manufacturer's directions.
4. Transfer to an airtight container and stir in pistachios. Freeze for at least 4 hours. Remove from freezer about 15 minutes before serving.

Matcha Green Tea, Almond and Macadamia Nut Ice Cream

This light and smooth ice cream enriched with almond butter and sweetened with rice syrup is a vegan version of the now-omnipresent matcha green tea ice cream. Matcha green tea in itself is a gold mine of antioxidants, so enjoy all the health benefits this tasty and refined dessert has to offer.

MAKES 6 TO 8 SERVINGS

- Blender
- Ice cream maker

3¼ cups	plain almond milk	800 mL
3 tbsp	almond butter	45 mL
5 tbsp	matcha green tea	75 mL
5 tbsp	rice syrup	75 mL
2 tbsp	chopped unsalted macadamia nuts	30 mL

Tip

This ice cream is perfect with a raspberry coulis, black sesame seeds or sprinkled with puffed rice.

Variation

For an even softer combination, replace the macadamia nuts with 1¾ oz (50 g) vegan white chocolate, chopped.

1. In blender, combine almond milk, almond butter, matcha and rice syrup; blend until smooth.
2. Churn in ice cream maker according to manufacturer's directions.
3. Transfer to an airtight container and stir in macadamia nuts. Freeze for at least 5 hours. Remove ice cream from freezer about 15 minutes before serving.

Ice Cream Sundae

A dish of light and smooth soft-serve ice cream topped with caramel, chocolate or strawberry sauce: decadence couldn't be simpler. This classic American recipe revisited as a vegan and organic version is just as tasty as the original.

MAKES 4 SERVINGS

- Ice cream maker
- Pastry bag, fitted with large star tip

3½ oz	plain soy yogurt	100 g
1¼ cups	soy cream	300 mL
6 tbsp	plain almond milk	90 mL
5 tbsp	light cane sugar	75 mL
1½ tsp	vanilla extract	7 mL

ACCOMPANIMENTS

Coconut or caramel nectar and chopped peanuts

Chocolate sauce and slivered almonds

Red berry coulis and candied cherries

Vegan whipped cream

1. In a small saucepan, over medium heat, whisk together soy yogurt, soy cream, almond milk, sugar and vanilla until sugar is dissolved. Let cool, then transfer to a bowl and refrigerate until chilled.

2. Churn in ice cream maker according to manufacturer's directions.

3. Pour a small amount of coconut nectar or sauce into the bottom of 4 ice cream cups or bowls.

4. When ice cream has completely set, transfer to pastry bag. Squeeze into ice cream cups and pour more nectar or sauce on top. Top with accompaniments as desired. Serve immediately, as this ice cream melts quickly!

Raspberry Frozen Yogurt

Light and smooth frozen yogurt is one of my favorites. It's easy to make a vegan version using soy yogurt and vegan cream. Frozen yogurt is not too sweet and is very refreshing in summertime. This version is marbled with raspberry coulis for a gourmet touch, but you can customize your own frozen yogurt with other ingredients.

MAKES 4 TO 6 SERVINGS

- Electric mixer (optional)
- Ice cream maker

³/₄ cup	confectioners' (icing) sugar	175 mL
21 oz	plain soy yogurt, well chilled	600 g
⁵/₄ cup + 2 tbsp	soy cream, well chilled	200 mL
3¹/₂ oz	frozen raspberries	100 g
2 tbsp	agave syrup	30 mL
2 tbsp	hot water	30 mL

Variations

Replace the raspberry coulis with fresh mango or strawberry coulis, lemon curd or homemade vegan dulce de leche.

For children or ice pop fans, spoon frozen yogurt into ice pop molds after adding the coulis and freeze for at least 5 hours.

1. In a medium bowl, using electric mixer or a whisk, beat sugar, soy yogurt and soy cream for a few minutes.

2. Churn in ice cream maker according to manufacturer's directions. (It will probably set more quickly than classic ice cream.)

3. In a bowl, mash together frozen raspberries, agave syrup and water, making a frozen coulis. Transfer frozen yogurt to an airtight container, pour raspberry coulis on top and mix gently to lightly marble frozen yogurt. Freeze for 2 to 3 hours before serving.

Pineapple Lime Sorbet

In summertime I swear by sorbets. The more tart and refreshing they are, the more I enjoy them. Fans of tart and tropical flavors will be delighted by this explosive combination of pineapple and lime. All you need to make a good sorbet are water, fruit and cane sugar!

MAKES 4 SERVINGS

- Blender
- Ice cream maker

²/₃ cup	water	150 mL
7 tbsp	light cane sugar	100 mL
1 lb	peeled pineapple, cut into chunks	500 g
5 tbsp	freshly squeezed lime juice	75 mL

Tip

No ice cream maker? No problem! Make a delicious, drinkable slushy or granita instead. Prepare the sugar syrup as directed in step 1 and chill. Freeze pineapple, then blend with lime juice and sugar syrup. Serve immediately in glasses with wide straws.

1. In a small saucepan, over medium heat, stir water and sugar until sugar is dissolved.
2. In blender, combine sugar syrup, pineapple and lime juice; blend until smooth. Refrigerate until chilled.
3. Churn in ice cream maker according to manufacturer's directions.
4. Transfer to an airtight container and freeze for at least 5 hours. Remove sorbet from freezer 15 minutes before serving, so that it is soft enough to scoop into balls.

Mango Melon Sorbet with Lemon Zest

For this sorbet, I combined my two favorite sorbet flavors with a touch of lemon for a deliciously tart note. The result is a sunny sorbet that makes you feel like you're on vacation. The advantage of this recipe is that it is so easy to make.

MAKES 4 TO 6 SERVINGS

- Blender
- Ice cream maker

7 tbsp	water	100 mL
5 tbsp + 1 tsp	light cane sugar	80 mL
11 oz	peeled melon (cantaloupe, honeydew, canary, etc.)	300 g
7 oz	peeled mango, coarsely chopped	200 g
1½ tsp	grated lemon zest	7 mL
1 tbsp	freshly squeezed lemon juice	15 mL

Tips

This sorbet is perfect with fresh fruit salad or melon balls and a few mint leaves.

Frozen fruit can be used instead of fresh fruit.

1. In a saucepan, over medium heat, stir water and sugar until sugar is dissolved.
2. In blender, combine sugar syrup, melon and mango; blend until very smooth. Add lemon zest and juice; blend to incorporate.
3. Churn in ice cream maker according to manufacturer's directions.
4. Transfer to an airtight container and freeze for at least 5 hours. Remove sorbet from freezer 15 minutes before serving, so that it is soft enough to scoop into balls.

Tomato, Strawberry and Basil Sorbet

A combination that is on its way to becoming a classic, and a recipe I never get tired of making, this sorbet's ripe fruits, bursting with sunshine and flavor, make it a real delight!

- Ice cream maker

10 oz	tomatoes, peeled, seeded and chopped	280 g
8 oz	strawberries, chopped	220 g
1¼ cups	water	300 mL
½ cup	light cane sugar	120 mL
2 tsp	chopped fresh basil	10 mL
⅛ tsp	vanilla extract	0.5 mL

Variations

Not a fan of basil? Replace it with fresh mint, which goes beautifully with tomatoes and strawberries.

Hankering for an extra-thirst-quenching sorbet? Replace the tomato with the same weight of watermelon (but do not cook the watermelon in the saucepan).

1. In a large saucepan, combine tomatoes and strawberries. Add water and sugar and stir over medium heat until sugar is dissolved. Cook over low heat for 5 minutes or until tomatoes are soft. Stir in basil. Let cool, then transfer to a bowl and refrigerate until chilled.

2. Churn in ice cream maker according to manufacturer's directions.

3. Transfer to an airtight container and freeze for at least 5 hours. Remove sorbet from freezer 15 minutes before serving, so that it is soft enough to scoop into balls.

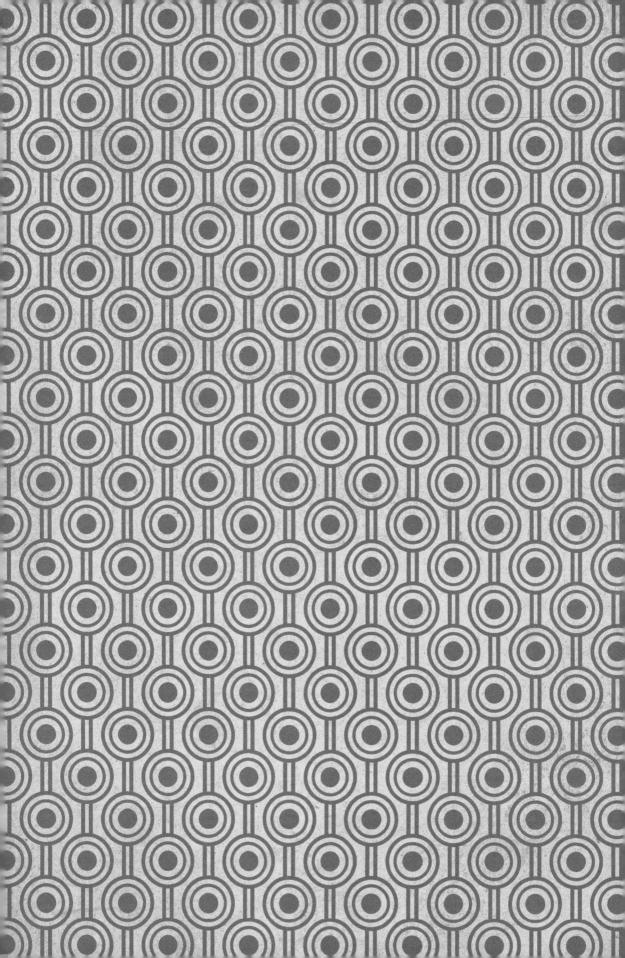

Ice Pops, Bars and Cones

Rainbow Rockets

These fruity ice pops dazzle the eye and are sure to please children of all ages. All you need is a little patience to achieve this pastel rainbow effect.

- Ice pop molds
- Immersion blender

LAYER 1

²/₃ cup	vegan cream or vegan yogurt	150 mL
2 tsp	agave syrup	10 mL
1 tsp	grated lemon zest	5 mL
1 tsp	freshly squeezed lemon juice	5 mL

LAYER 2

²/₃ cup	vegan cream or vegan yogurt	150 mL
1 tsp	agave syrup	5 mL
¹/₃ cup	chopped mango	75 mL

LAYER 3

²/₃ cup	vegan cream or vegan yogurt	150 mL
2 tsp	agave syrup	10 mL
2	strawberries	2

LAYER 4

²/₃ cup	vegan cream or vegan yogurt	150 mL
2 tsp	agave syrup	10 mL
3 tbsp	raspberries	45 mL

LAYER 5

²/₃ cup	vegan cream or vegan yogurt	150 mL
2 tsp	agave syrup	10 mL
1 tbsp	blueberries	15 mL

1. *Layer 1:* In a bowl, whisk together cream, agave syrup, lemon zest and lemon juice. Pour into ice pop molds, dividing equally. Freeze for 30 to 40 minutes. The first layer should be firm enough so that you can pour the next layer on top without mixing them together.

2. *Layer 2:* In a tall cup, combine cream, agave syrup and mango; using an immersion blender, purée until smooth. Pour into molds on top of first layer. Freeze for 30 to 40 minutes or until firm.

3. *Layers 3 through 5:* Repeat with the remaining ingredients, puréeing each layer separately, and pour into molds once previously layer is firm. Insert sticks when layer 3 starts to set. After adding layer 5, freeze for 4 to 5 hours, until solid. Run mold under a stream of hot water to remove ice pops.

Smoothie Ice Pops

How do you encourage children to eat their spinach? Simple! Just turn it into a smoothie ice pop. I leave it to you to choose between these tasty green or pink treats (or the two-color variation).

MAKES 4 ICE POPS

- **Blender**
- **Ice pop molds**

½	banana	½
¼	mango, chopped (1 oz/30 g)	¼
1¼ cups	vegan milk or water	300 mL
1 tbsp	cashew or almond butter	15 mL
1 to 2 tsp	agave syrup (optional)	5 to 10 mL

GREEN SMOOTHIE VERSION

1 cup	packed trimmed spinach	250 mL

PINK SMOOTHIE VERSION

½ cup	raspberries	125 mL

Tip

You can make ice pops out of any kind of smoothie, using the same recipe. Choose the creamiest recipes with ingredients that will set well (so the water does not separate from the fibers).

1. In blender, combine banana, mango, milk, cashew butter and agave syrup to taste; blend until smooth.
2. For the green version, add spinach and blend until smooth; for the pink version, add raspberries and blend until smooth.
3. Pour into ice pop molds, dividing equally. Freeze for 4 to 5 hours, until solid, inserting sticks when partially frozen. (If using sticks with covers, you can insert them at the beginning.) Run mold under a stream of hot water to remove ice pops.

Variation

For two-colored ice pops, prepare the green smoothie and fill 8 ice pop molds halfway. Freeze for about 90 minutes, until firm. Prepare the pink smoothie, then pour into molds on top of green smoothie. Return to freezer and let set for 4 to 5 hours, inserting sticks when partially firm (or at the beginning if using sticks with covers).

Banana Blueberry Milkshake Pops

A few minutes are all you need to prepare these super-creamy little ice pops. Each one is a serving of vegan milkshake, stocked with antioxidants and frozen on a stick — a simple way to make healthy cuisine more fun!

MAKES ABOUT 8 ICE POPS		

- **Blender**
- **Ice pop molds**

3¹⁄₂ oz	banana, cut into pieces	100 g
¹⁄₃ cup	blueberries	75 mL
1²⁄₃ cups	almond milk	400 mL
2 tbsp	agave syrup	30 mL
¹⁄₈ tsp	vanilla bean powder	0.5 mL

Variations

Strawberries or raspberries are a perfect substitution for blueberries.

Add a few dark chocolate chips when pouring the mixture into the molds.

1. In blender, combine banana, blueberries, almond milk, agave syrup and vanilla powder; blend until smooth.

2. Pour into ice pop molds, dividing equally. Freeze for at least 5 hours, until firm, inserting sticks when partially frozen. (If using sticks with covers, you can insert them at the beginning.) Run mold under a stream of hot water to remove ice pops.

Peach Pie Ice Cream Pops

A pastry-inspired treat featuring fresh fruit, rich cream and a biscuit layer.

- Preheat oven to 325°F (160°C)
- Baking sheet, lined with parchment paper
- Ice pop molds

BISCUIT CRUST

2 tbsp	light cane sugar	30 mL
1 tbsp	neutral vegetable oil	15 mL
1½ oz	oat flour	45 g
2 tsp	almond milk	10 mL
2 tbsp	vegan cream	30 mL

ICE CREAM POPS

¾ cup + 2 tbsp	soy cream	200 mL
2 tbsp	agave syrup	30 mL
1 tbsp	cashew butter	15 mL
½ tsp	vanilla extract	2 mL
7 oz	yellow peaches, peeled and diced	200 g

1. *Biscuit Crust:* In a bowl, stir together sugar and oil. Add half the flour, then almond milk. Blend thoroughly. Add the remaining flour and knead into dough. Shape dough into a cylinder, then press onto prepared baking sheet into a rectangle about 5 by 2 inches (12.5 by 5 cm).

2. Bake in preheated oven for 5 minutes. Let cool, then crumble into small pieces in a bowl. Stir in vegan cream. Set aside.

3. *Ice Cream Pops:* In a bowl, whisk together soy cream, agave syrup, cashew butter and vanilla extract. Place peaches in ice pop molds, packing them down, then pour in soy cream mixture, leaving about ½ inch (1 cm) of space at the top of the molds.

4. Freeze for about 2 hours, until starting to set. Insert sticks, top with biscuit crust and freeze for 3 more hours, until solid. Run mold under a stream of hot water to remove ice pops.

Orange Mango Striped Ice Pops

Vitamin-packed, low-sugar ice pops that are fun to eat, economical and easy to make — what more could you ask?

MAKES 6 ICE POPS

- Immersion blender (optional)
- Ice pop molds

1 cup	mango nectar (minimum 40% fruit)	250 mL
3/4 cup + 2 tbsp	freshly squeezed orange juice (about 3 oranges)	200 mL
3 tbsp	soy cream	45 mL
1 tbsp	agave syrup	15 mL

Tip

You can make many thin layers if you wish, or vary the thickness to make irregular stripes. It's up to your imagination and how much time you have!

1. Pour mango nectar into a glass measuring cup or bowl with a pouring lip.

2. In another glass measuring cup or bowl with a pouring lip, using a whisk or immersion blender, mix together orange juice, soy cream and agave syrup.

3. Pour a small quantity of one of the two mixtures into ice pop molds to make the first layer. Freeze for about 45 minutes (refrigerate extra mixtures while ice pops freeze). The layer should be firm enough so that you can pour the next layer on top without them mixing together, but it does not have to be completely frozen.

4. Pour a second layer of identical thickness, using the other mixture. Freeze for about 45 minutes. Continue in this way, alternating layers. Insert sticks when the middle layer starts to set. Once all the layers have set, let harden in freezer for 4 hours. Run mold under a stream of hot water to remove ice pops.

Cucumber Mojito Paletas

Paleta is the Spanish word for an ice pop. *Paleterias* are the little shops that sell these treats, which come in a rainbow of colors and flavors. *Paleterias* originated in Mexico but are also very popular in California. *Paletas* are more than just simple ice pops. Each *paleteria* has its own original and creative recipes. Here is a handcrafted version that combines lime, mint and cucumber in a very refreshing way.

MAKES ABOUT 10 ICE POPS

- Blender
- Ice pop molds

4½ oz	cucumber, cut into chunks	125 g
1¼ cups	water	300 mL
5 tbsp	agave syrup	75 mL
¼ cup	freshly squeezed lime juice	60 mL
1 tbsp	finely chopped mint leaves	15 mL
1½ oz	cucumber, slivered (optional)	45 g

Tip

Pour this mixture, without cucumber slivers, into ice cube trays and store in the freezer. For an ultra-fresh and tasty drink that's ready in the blink of an eye, pop 2 ice cubes into a glass of plain or sparkling water!

1. In blender, combine cucumber, water, agave syrup and lime juice; blend until smooth. Strain through a sieve to obtain a clear juice. Stir mint into juice.

2. If you like, add slivers of cucumber to the ice pop molds. Pour juice into the molds, dividing evenly. Freeze for 8 hours, until firm, inserting sticks when partially frozen. (If using sticks with covers, you can insert them at the beginning.) Run mold under a stream of hot water to remove ice pops.

Coconut Dark Chocolate Ice Cream Bars

This sinfully rich ice cream features a crunchy chocolate and shredded coconut coating. All you need are five fair-trade ingredients for a guilt-free frozen treat.

MAKES ABOUT 8 ICE CREAM BARS

- Blender
- Ice cream bar molds
- Double boiler

1	can (14 oz/400 mL) coconut milk	1
4 to 5 tbsp	agave syrup	60 to 75 mL
1 tsp	vanilla extract	5 mL
14 oz	dark chocolate, chopped	400 g
	Shredded sweetened or unsweetened coconut	

Tip

Store these ice cream bars in the freezer, wrapped in parchment paper in an airtight container, if you are not eating them immediately.

1. In blender, combine coconut milk, agave syrup to taste and vanilla; blend well.

2. Pour into ice cream bar molds with sticks and freeze until solid. Remove frozen ice cream bars from molds, then store in freezer.

3. Melt chocolate in double boiler and pour into a glass just wide enough to fit ice cream bars. Working quickly, dip frozen ice cream bars in chocolate, allow excess to drip off, then sprinkle with shredded coconut. Lay on parchment paper in an airtight container and return to freezer for 30 minutes.

Chocolate Praline Cones

These Italian-style ice cream cones look like they come from the ice cream shop. The cones are filled using a pastry bag. You can save time by preparing the vanilla ice cream ahead of time and flavoring it with chocolate and hazelnut butter at the last minute.

MAKES 6 CONES

- Ice cream maker
- Double boiler
- 2 plastic pastry bags, uncut
- Large pastry bag, fitted with large star tip

2 cups	soy cream	500 mL
1/3 cup	light cane sugar	75 mL
	Seeds from 1 vanilla bean pod	
2 tbsp	unsweetened cocoa powder	30 mL
2 tbsp	toasted hazelnut butter	30 mL
2 tbsp	praline powder	30 mL

CONES

3 1/2 oz	dark baking chocolate	100 g
6	Homemade Cones (page 80)	6
1/4 cup	chopped hazelnuts	60 mL

1. In a saucepan, over high heat, whisk together soy cream, sugar and vanilla seeds until sugar is dissolved. Let cool, then transfer to a bowl and refrigerate until chilled.

2. Churn in ice cream maker according to manufacturer's directions.

3. *Cones:* Melt chocolate in double boiler, then dip edges of cones in chocolate (or use a small rubber spatula to spread chocolate on edges of cones). Sprinkle chopped hazelnuts on chocolate. Place in refrigerator to let chocolate harden.

4. Divide vanilla ice cream equally between two bowls. Add cocoa powder to one bowl and hazelnut butter to the other bowl. Stir with a rubber spatula.

5. Transfer each mixture to an uncut pastry bag, seal bags and freeze for 30 minutes.

6. Remove bags from freezer, cut off tips and insert both bags into pastry bag with star tip. Fill cones and sprinkle with praline powder. Serve immediately.

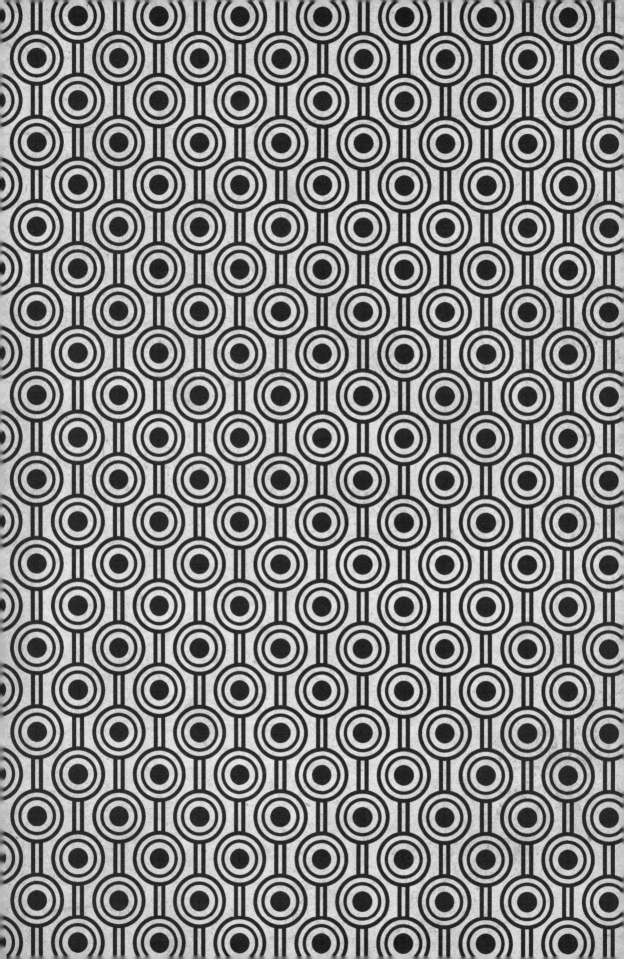

Delicious
Frozen Desserts

Chocolate, Coffee and Vanilla Neapolitan

Easier to make than it looks, this Neapolitan is ideal after a feast with family or friends. Just take it out of the freezer and decorate it for a superb, creamy and decadent dessert that's ready in the blink of an eye.

MAKES 8 TO 10 SERVINGS

- Ice cream maker
- 8- by 4-inch (20 by 10 cm) metal loaf pan, lined with plastic wrap
- Double boiler

4 cups	soy cream	1 L
½ cup	light cane sugar	125 mL
	Seeds from 2 vanilla bean pods	
2 tbsp	unsweetened cocoa powder	30 mL
2 tbsp	instant coffee granules	30 mL
2 tsp	water	10 mL
10 oz	dark chocolate, chopped	300 g

DECORATIONS

Melted chocolate or chocolate sauce

Dark chocolate shavings

Caramel topping

Chopped hazelnuts

Tip

As the quantity of ingredients is a little higher than in other recipes, this ice cream will likely need to churn longer in the ice cream maker.

1. In a large saucepan, over medium heat, whisk together soy cream, sugar and vanilla seeds until sugar is dissolved. Let cool, then transfer to a bowl and refrigerate until chilled.

2. Churn in ice cream maker according to manufacturer's directions.

3. Transfer one-third of the ice cream into prepared pan, spreading and smoothing top; place in freezer immediately.

4. Divide the remaining ice cream equally between two bowls. In one bowl, mix in cocoa powder with a rubber spatula, then place bowl in freezer.

5. In a small bowl or cup, mix instant coffee and water, then pour mixture into the other bowl and blend thoroughly. Place bowl in freezer.

6. Melt chocolate in double boiler. When ice cream in loaf pan is very hard, spread a thin layer of melted chocolate on top. Let harden for 1 minute. Spread coffee ice cream on top, then freeze until very hard. Repeat with the remaining melted chocolate and the chocolate ice cream. Freeze for 4 hours, until solid.

7. Remove Neapolitan from freezer 10 minutes before serving and transfer from loaf pan to a plate. Decorate it with your choice of decorations, then slice it at the last minute.

Black Sesame Ice Cream with Raspberry Coulis

Black sesame in dessert recipes is my latest passion. Just as they did with matcha green tea powder, the Japanese are setting the tone for us with their many recipes for pudding, ice cream and cookies that highlight the intense flavor of black sesame seeds. In this recipe, black sesame paste is mixed into smooth molded ice cream for a chic and visually impressive dessert.

MAKES 6 SERVINGS

- Ice cream maker
- Miniature Bundt pans or other miniature fluted pans

2 cups	soy cream	500 mL
3 tbsp	black sesame paste	45 mL
3 tbsp	rice syrup	45 mL
3 tbsp	plain soy yogurt	45 mL
1/4 tsp	vanilla bean powder	1 mL
1 cup	raspberry coulis	250 mL
6	raspberries	6

Tips

Black sesame paste can be found in organic form on the internet or in specialty stores. If you have a high-powered blender, you can also make your own paste by blending black sesame seeds for a long time until a paste forms.

As an alternative, look for black sesame cream in organic food stores. It is a blend of 50% blond and 50% black sesame seeds. Its flavor is not as pronounced as that of black sesame paste, but it is perfectly suited to this recipe.

1. In a bowl, whisk together soy cream, sesame paste, rice syrup, yogurt and vanilla powder.
2. Churn in ice cream maker according to manufacturer's directions.
3. Pour into Bundt pans and freeze for 6 hours, until sold.
4. Unmold onto plates or a platter and serve with raspberry coulis in the center and a raspberry on top.

Apple Cinnamon Granita

This granita, with its wintertime flavors, is astonishing — it tastes like delicious spiced applesauce, but with a frosty texture that melts in the mouth instantly and leaves you with just one desire: to dig in your spoon again!

MAKES 8 SERVINGS

6	cardamom pods	6
¼ cup	raw cane sugar	60 mL
½ tsp	ground cinnamon	2 mL
4 cups	unfiltered apple juice	1 L
1 tsp	vanilla extract	5 mL

1. Open cardamom pods and empty seeds into a medium saucepan. Add sugar, cinnamon, apple juice and vanilla. Stir over medium heat for at least 5 minutes to completely dissolve sugar. Strain mixture through a sieve into a metal bowl or metal cake pan. (A metal container is a better conductor of cold, ideal for helping the granita set.) Let cool.

2. Freeze mixture for 2 hours, until set, then scrape it with a fork, taking care to scrape the sides of the bowl or pan as well. Scrape mixture every hour, or every half hour, until granita forms. Setting time will vary according to temperature of freezer. Once granita has completely set, store it in an airtight container. Serve at the last minute, as it melts very quickly.

Orange Blossom and Pistachio Mysteries

This frozen dessert is one of my favorites, featuring rich ice cream scented with orange blossom and a decadent pistachio nut center. Reminiscent of Middle Eastern pastry, it's an exotic voyage that begins with the first bite! The good news is that you can prepare it without an ice cream maker.

MAKES 4 SERVINGS

- Blender
- Ice cream maker (optional)
- 4 hemisphere molds (optional)
- Baking sheet, lined with parchment paper

1½ cups	raw cashews (6 oz/175 g)	375 mL
⅓ cup	light cane sugar	75 mL
¾ cup + 2 tbsp	almond milk	200 mL
1 tbsp	orange blossom water	15 mL

FILLING

¼ cup	pistachios, finely chopped	60 mL
1 tbsp	praline powder	15 mL
2 tbsp	rice syrup	30 mL
½ tsp	vanilla extract	2 mL

COATING

⅓ cup	pistachios, finely chopped	75 mL
¾ cup + 2 tbsp	raspberry coulis	200 mL

1. In a bowl, soak cashews in water overnight.

2. Drain cashews and transfer to blender. Add sugar, almond milk and orange blossom water; blend into a thick and very smooth cream.

3. Transfer to an airtight container and freeze, stirring cream every hour for about 5 hours. (Or churn in ice cream maker according to manufacturer's directions.)

4. *Filling:* In a bowl, combine pistachios, praline powder, rice syrup and vanilla. Set aside.

Option 1

5. If using hemisphere molds, pack ice cream into molds, filling three-quarters full. Set aside some ice cream. Freeze all for 1 hour, then add 1½ tsp (7 mL) filling to the center and pack down the filling. Seal the mysteries by packing molds with the remaining ice cream. Freeze until hemispheres are sufficiently set to be removed from molds but are still slightly soft.

6. *Coating:* Place hemispheres on prepared baking sheet and cover with chopped pistachios. Serve with raspberry coulis.

Option 2

5. If you don't have molds, you need to make an ice cream that is sufficiently dense but still soft enough to be molded by hand. Form 4 balls of ice cream, dig a small well in the center of each and add 1½ tsp (7 mL) filling. Seal the balls by hand and reform them carefully using your hands.

6. *Coating:* Place balls on prepared baking sheet and cover with chopped pistachios. Serve with raspberry coulis.

Ice Cream Sandwiches

Here's a great American classic, revisited in an enticing new way with caramelized pecan ice cream.

- Preheat oven to 325°F (160°C)
- Rectangular cookie cutter
- Baking sheets, lined with parchment paper
- Rectangular pan

COOKIES

1/4 cup	neutral vegetable oil	60 mL
2 tbsp	almond butter	30 mL
2 tbsp	unsweetened cocoa powder	30 mL
3 tbsp + 1 tsp	water	50 mL
7 oz	all-purpose flour	200 g
1/4 tsp	salt	1 mL

ICE CREAM

1/3 cup	chopped pecans	75 mL
1 1/2 tbsp	light cane sugar	22 mL
1 tbsp	water	15 mL
1/2	recipe Vanilla Ice Cream (page 84)	1/2

1. *Cookies:* In a bowl, whisk together sugar, oil and almond butter. Add cocoa powder and water. Sift flour and salt over the mixture, then blend thoroughly.

2. Form dough into 2 balls, then roll them out to rectangles no more than 1/4 inch (0.5 cm) thick. Using cookie cutter, cut dough into 20 rectangles. Place on prepared baking sheets, spacing 1 inch (2.5 cm) apart.

3. Bake in preheated oven for 5 minutes. Let cookies cool on a rack, then store in an airtight container.

4. *Ice Cream:* Line a baking sheet with fresh parchment paper. Place pecans in a skillet with sugar. Add water and let pecans caramelize over medium heat, stirring constantly. Transfer to baking sheet, separate pieces carefully and let cool.

5. Transfer ice cream from ice cream maker to rectangular pan, add pecans and mix together. Let set in freezer for at least 6 hours or until ice cream is very hard.

6. Remove ice cream from freezer and cut into rectangles about 1/2 inch (1 cm) thick and the same dimensions as the cookies. Assemble sandwiches just before serving.

Raspberry and Lemon Crumble Miniature Logs

This dessert log features an easy raspberry sorbet and simple coconut milk ice cream. A few ingredients and a little effort are all it takes for a result worthy of a gourmet chef!

- Blender
- 6 individual loaf pans (or 2 small cake pans)
- Baking sheet, lined with parchment paper

7 oz	frozen raspberries	210 g
3 tbsp	water	45 mL
3 tbsp	agave syrup	45 mL
1	can (14 oz/400 mL) coconut milk	1
1/3 cup	light cane sugar	75 mL

CRUMBLE

1 1/2 oz	whole wheat flour (preferably einkorn wheat)	45 g
2 tbsp	muscovado sugar	30 mL
1 tbsp	neutral vegetable oil	15 mL
1 tbsp	almond butter	15 mL
1 1/2 tsp	finely grated lemon zest	7 mL

Tip

You can also decorate with a raspberry coulis for a more fruity effect.

1. In blender, combine raspberries, water and agave syrup; blend until smooth. Pour into loaf pans. Freeze for about 30 minutes. (This layer should be hard enough that you can pour the second layer on top without mixing them together.)

2. In a saucepan, over medium heat, stir coconut milk and cane sugar until sugar is dissolved. Let cool. Spread on top of raspberry layer and return to freezer for about 1 hour.

3. Preheat oven to 325°F (160°C).

4. *Crumble:* In a bowl, combine flour, muscovado sugar, oil and almond butter; mix with your fingertips until crumbly. Spread mixture on prepared baking sheet. Bake for 5 minutes. Let cool completely.

5. Spread three-quarters of crumble on ice cream layer. Press down lightly to make crumble stick to ice cream.

6. Remove miniature logs from freezer 5 to 10 minutes before serving, remove them from pans, then decorate them with the remaining crumble and lemon zest.

Vanilla Pear Hazelnut Biscuit Log

For many people, the Yule log is an essential part of the holiday meal at Christmastime. Here's an easy recipe that takes the drudgery out of preparing it, in three easy steps, featuring a simple vanilla ice cream, gently caramelized pears and a hazelnut biscuit crust.

MAKES 10 TO 12 SERVINGS

- Preheat oven to 350°F (180°C)
- Dessert log mold
- 2 baking sheets, lined with parchment paper

1	recipe Vanilla Ice Cream (page 84)	1

BISCUIT CRUST

2 tbsp	hazelnut butter	30 mL
2 tbsp	neutral vegetable oil	30 mL
3 tbsp + 1 tsp	raw cane sugar	50 mL
1/4 cup	plain soy yogurt	60 mL
1 1/2 tsp	baking powder	7 mL
3 1/2 oz	all-purpose flour	100 g

CARAMELIZED PEARS

1/4 cup	sugar	60 mL
3 tbsp	water	45 mL
4	pears, peeled and quartered, quarters halved lengthwise	4

DECORATION

Caramel topping

Praline powder

1. Once your vanilla ice cream has finished churning in the ice cream maker, transfer it to the dessert log mold and freeze for 1 hour.

2. *Biscuit Crust:* Meanwhile, in a bowl, whisk together hazelnut butter and oil. Whisk in sugar and soy yogurt, then baking powder. Add flour and mix thoroughly with a rubber spatula.

3. Spread dough on a prepared baking sheet, over an area slightly larger than that of the mold. Smooth dough with a moistened hand (dough is sticky).

4. Bake in preheated oven for about 12 minutes. Surface should be golden. Let cool.

5. *Caramelized Pears:* Meanwhile, in a medium skillet, combine sugar and water, then place pear pieces in skillet. Cook over high heat for about 10 minutes, watching pears carefully but not touching them. When pears have just begun to caramelize (when you first smell caramel), turn them over and reduce heat to medium. Cook for 5 minutes, turning pears over once or twice. When they start to turn golden, increase to high heat and let caramelize for 1 to 2 minutes, stirring gently. Pear pieces should not brown.

6. Place pears one by one on another prepared baking sheet, separate them and let them cool completely.

7. When ice cream begins to firm, lay caramelized pear pieces on top to cover surface. Cut biscuit crust to the size of the base of the mold and place on top of pear pieces. Press down lightly to make biscuit stick. Freeze for at least 5 hours.

8. Remove log from freezer 10 minutes before serving. Transfer from mold to a large platter and decorate with caramel topping and praline powder.

Frozen Mini Layer Cakes

Halfway between cake and ice cream, this recipe is perfect as a dessert or an elegant snack. This version features blood orange juice, but you can make it with any other kind of fruit juice you like.

- Blender
- 2 baking sheets, lined with parchment paper
- Two 2³/₄- to 3¹/₄-inch (7 to 8 cm) metal pastry rings

ICE CREAM

7 oz	cashews	200 g
1 cup	blood orange juice	250 mL
3 to 4 tbsp	agave syrup	45 to 60 mL
¹/₂ tsp	vanilla extract	2 mL

CAKE

¹/₂ cup	light cane sugar	125 mL
¹/₂ cup	plain soy yogurt	125 mL
5 tbsp	neutral vegetable oil	75 mL
3 tbsp	unsweetened cocoa powder	45 mL
2 tsp	baking powder	10 mL
¹/₈ tsp	vanilla bean powder	0.5 mL
2 tbsp	vegan milk	30 mL
3¹/₂ oz	whole wheat flour, preferably einkorn wheat	100 g
¹/₄ tsp	salt	1 mL

Tip

Serve with melted chocolate and fresh fruit (such as a salad of oranges or other tart fruits, like raspberries or strawberries, depending on the season).

1. *Ice Cream:* In a bowl, soak cashews in water for 8 to 12 hours.

2. Drain cashews and transfer to blender. Add orange juice, agave syrup to taste and vanilla; blend until smooth. Freeze in an airtight container to chill (but do not freeze solid).

3. *Cake:* Preheat oven to 350°F (180°C).

4. In a large bowl, whisk together sugar, soy yogurt and oil. Add cocoa powder, baking powder and vanilla powder; stir well. Gradually incorporate milk, then sift flour with salt into batter and stir until combined. Spread mixture on a prepared baking sheet to a uniform thickness.

5. Bake for 15 minutes. Let cool. Using a metal pastry ring, cut out 6 cake rounds.

6. Place both pastry rings on another prepared baking sheet (or on a platter). Place a cake round inside each. Pour a similar thickness of ice cream into each ring. Add a second layer of cake, then a second layer of ice cream, and finish with the last layer of cake. Freeze for at least 4 hours. Insert a knife blade around the edge of the ring to remove the ice cream cake.

Library and Archives Canada Cataloguing in Publication

Laforêt, Marie, 1983-, author
    The best homemade vegan cheese & ice cream recipes / Marie Laforêt.

Includes index.
"Originally published under the titles *Fromages Vegan* ©2014, Éditions la Plage (Paris) and *25 Glaces Vegan* ©2015, Éditions la Plage (Paris)"—Title page verso.
ISBN 978-0-7788-0543-4 (paperback)

1. Vegan cooking. 2. Cheesemaking. 3. Ice cream, ices, etc.
4. Non-dairy frozen desserts. 5. Milk-free diet—Recipes. 6. Cookbooks—
I. Title. II. Title: Homemade vegan cheese & ice cream recipes.
III. Laforêt, Marie, 1983- . Fromages vegan. English.
IV. Laforêt, Marie, 1983- . 25 glaces vegan. English.

TX837.L33 2016   641.5'636   C2016-902966-2

Index